JOINING
JESUS
SHOW ME HOW

At its core, discipleship is the art of imitation. In the first-century Galilee, a time and place where discipleship flourished, a disciple learned how to experience the love of God and navigate through life by having someone show them how it's done. Greg Finke has captured this authentic spirit of discipleship in a very practical and succinct format that is sure to help individuals, and from there, even whole congregations, return to the Hebraic way of showing and imitating.

—Dr. Chad Yeshayahu Foster, Messianic Rabbi Columbus, Indiana

For those of us who need help with "Follow me!" we now have "Show Me How." This is really good work by Greg. He just has a way of putting truth on the bottom shelf for easy reach. This how-to is great for personal or group consumption. I know I plan to do both!

—Reggie McNeal, author of *Get Off Your Donkey!* and *Kingdom Come*

In a time when everyone is calling for more effective discipling, Greg Finke actually shows us how to do it. Greg brings clarity and simplicity to the how-to of discipling people to be everyday missionaries. If your church strategy includes disciple making, read this book!

—Will Mancini, Founder of Younique, author of *God Dreams*

What I love about this book is that it begins and ends with Jesus: mimicking his moves, trusting his words and following his lead to help you fold those you love into a life of seeking after God's kingdom activity. *Joining Jesus—Show Me How* is an essential handbook for learning what it truly means to disciple others, not just because of its great clarity and practicality but also because it takes you by the hand and walks you alongside the Savior.

—Matt Popovits, Pastor, Our Saviour, New York City; author of *Tough Call: A Little Book on Making Big Decisions*

Jesus directed his disciples to replicate themselves by making disciples. But how? Greg Finke provides sound insights and heartfelt encouragement to guide everyday disciples toward this calling, all by directing us to Jesus and his gracious gift of guidance.

—Dr. David J. Peter, Chairman of the Department of Practical Theology, Concordia Seminary, St. Louis, MO

Greg and Susan Finke write what they live. *Joining Jesus—Show Me How* will encourage, enlighten and enable you to show others how to follow Jesus.

—Jeff Meyer, PLI Missional Leader; Lead Navigator, Auxano

In his first book, Greg Finke dared to say that Jesus is alive and well and working in and through relationships in the world. In his long-awaited follow up book, he shows us how to disciple one another so that others can see what a life of following Jesus looks like.

—Heather Choate Davis, author, theologian and co-founder of icktank

In an approach not only biblical but practical and accessible for every Christian, Greg takes us back to an ancient method much needed in the clamor of today's busyness. Having recommended Greg's initial outing, I'm glad to see this hands-on sequel!

—Bill Woolsey, Executive Director and President, The Five Two Network

Starting with Jesus as our example, Greg rips the act of discipling from solely the professional ranks and empowers the average Christian to live out this calling. I would encourage you to accept the invitation to join Jesus in discipling everyday missionaries!

—Kurt Buchholz, President and CEO, Lutheran Hour Ministries

Greg's book embodies Jesus' pattern for disciple-making by laying out a biblical, Spirit-filled, Spirit-led, doable and reproducible way to help others to become more like Jesus, join Jesus on his mission and lead others to do the same. I devoured his book and am already fine-tuning my following of Christ as a result. What a gift and treasure this book will be to all those seeking to make disciples.

—Dr. Scott Rische, PLI International

Greg has the uncanny ability to make the act of discipleship understandable and practical. Thanks, Greg, for another great reminder of how to live out my calling.

—Dr. Donald Christian, President and Chief Executive Officer, Concordia University Texas

Greg beautifully communicates how we live out those two words spoken by Jesus: "Follow me." Following Jesus isn't easy, and I don't think it was intended to be. However, this book gives clarity and direction to those who seek to follow him. Greg's words get us moving. They pick us up and encourage us for the adventure ahead. After reading this book, I felt refreshed and ready, not only to lead, but also to walk alongside others in this mission.

—Tanner Olson, spoken word poet and creator of writtentospeak.com

My dear brother and friend has once again inspired me with this new book. It is a beautiful successor to *Joining Jesus on His Mission* and gives a much needed, foundational understanding of what we now get to do as freely-saved disciples of Christ. It is a must for every Bible Study, small group and especially new member or introduction to Christianity class. Let the adventure begin!

—Rev. Dr. David P. E. Maier, President, The Michigan District, LCMS

As Greg Finke points out, most Christians are trained to "come and sit." Come and sit in worship…in class…in meetings, etc. Most leaders feel fortunate when 20%-30% of the congregation actually does come and sit on Sundays. "Come and sit" does not release the baptized people of God to be the missionaries where they live, work and play. Greg Finke is raising the bar. Sounding the alarm. Pointing the way. All with a smile in his heart and an invitation on his lips. We highly recommend this book!

—Gail and Jock Ficken, PLI Executive Leaders

Discipling has become a buzzword that seems all but impossible to fulfill, like a skill reserved for the ultra-talented keynote speaker you pay to see at a conference. This book dashes that misconception! Greg has a way of cutting through the conference clutter and taking you back to the heart of biblical discipleship. It rips discipleship out of the clutches of another cliché conference and puts it back into the hands of the everyday Christian in a way that leaves you saying, *I could actually do that!* If you are a pastor or ministry leader, this is more than just a great resource for your people; it is a great resource for you. This book is a reminder of how simple discipling was always meant to be.

—Matt Peeples, Pastor, Speaker, and Church Plant Trainer for the New Jersey District of the LCMS.

As Christians we are privileged to live in the midst of the Second Reformation. The First Reformation gave the Word to the people, but the Ministry has remained primarily in the control of the clergy. Today both Word and Ministry are being given to the people. How? By simply making first-century disciples of Jesus in the 21st century. Greg Finke's two books have become for me the most clear and powerful books to take part in this Second Reformation. I heartily encourage their reading.

—Rev. Dr. Paul Borg, Indianapolis, IN

Greg reminds us about Jesus' great invitation to follow him and to learn the simple but powerful art of discipling others. This is where a Gospel movement begins and how God's heart's desire of salvation is satisfied. Greg gives a huge dose of grace for the discipling journey!

—Michael W. Newman, author of *Gospel DNA: Five Markers of a Flourishing Church*

Discipling got ya stumped? No more, friend. The "how" is here. Welcome to how-land! Greg has us howling one minute—he's funny—and hopping on board the next. His signature calm and adventuresome spirit pull us into playing "Follow the Leader' with Jesus. Greg's approach is so simple and appealing I can read it on Monday and do it on Tuesday!

—Phyllis Wallace, writer, broadcaster and former host of the "Woman to Woman" radio show

Greg Finke has captured a sense of the heart of God that inspires and helps focus the disciple's life. By articulating the simple truth that "God wants his world (and his people) back," Greg sets our minds and hearts on a mission that is God's mission.

—Rev. Dr. Paul Linnemann, President of the Northwest District LCMS

Simple. That is what Greg is saying. It is simple. Making disciples of Jesus is simply doing what Jesus did: calling others to you, teaching them the basics, showing them how to live those basics with others and then releasing them to do the same. Use this book with your community to begin the exciting process of becoming disciple-making disciples.

—Rev. Paul Mueller, PhD Missiology; Executive Director, Center for Applied Lutheran Leadership, Concordia University-Portland, OR

Growing up in the "system," I was immersed in Scripture and taught the Church's doctrines, practices and traditions. But no one ever taught me how to disciple someone else. *Joining Jesus—Show Me How* will help anyone who had been blessed by the Gospel to begin discipling others to live in this hope that we have in Jesus.

—Mike Zimmer, Mission Facilitator, Northern Illinois District, LCMS

This book clarifies and simplifies our understanding of the disciple-making process. Jesus does the hard work that only the Son of God can do, and he invites us to join him in the process of showing the people of God how to participate in the mission of God as a daily lifestyle. And it's simple! This book has inspired me!

—Bob Fossum, Director of Family Ministry, Northwest District, LCMS

JOINING JESUS

SHOW ME HOW

How to Disciple
Everyday Missionaries

TENTH
POWER

ELGIN, IL · TYLER, TX

TENTHPOWERPUBLISHING
www.tenthpowerpublishing.com

Design by Inkwell Creative

Softcover ISBN 978-1-938840-15-9

e-book ISBN 978-1-938840-16-6

10 9 8 7 6 5 4 3 2 1

To my wife and children, who were showing me how to join Jesus

on his mission well before we had words to describe it.

TABLE OF CONTENTS

PART 1: REGAINING CLARITY AND SIMPLICITY FOR HOW JESUS DISCIPLES HIS FOLLOWERS IN THE GOSPELS

PART 2: CRAFTING YOUR DISCIPLING PLAN

FOREWORD

Among the myriad non-negotiables of the Triune God, two particularly stand out. The first, God loves his creation with all his heart and all his might. He will stop at nothing to restore it fully and wholly to himself. The second non-negotiable springs from the first: Though the business of restoring this fallen creation to its original beauty and perfection is God's alone, he chooses not to do his work alone. Because he loves all of his children with all of his heart, he desires that all of us join him on his mission.

The oft-called Great Commission of Matthew 28 then links these two non-negotiables together. The church most often understands these words, "Go and make disciples," to mean, "Jesus finished his work; it's now our turn." However, a little closer read of the Great Commission reveals that Jesus bookends his commission with, "All authority is given to me," and, "Lo I am with you always." In short, Jesus asks the church to disciple the nations with him, not for him. Greg Finke put it spot on in his first book, *Joining Jesus on His Mission.*

In *Joining Jesus—Show Me How,* Greg continues the conversation by unpacking our Lord's simple plan for being discipled by him and making disciples with him.

Jesus invited men and women to walk with him, live with him and learn of him as he walked with, lived with, and learned of his Father. That's how Jesus made disciples then, and that's how he makes them now. Discipleship takes place in relationship with our Lord and other people inside and outside the church. In fact, discipleship is all about relationship, growing deeper in our trust in the Lord and his Word by following him into a broken and abusive world desperate for his love.

Greg joined Jesus on his mission several years ago and has been walking the discipling road with Jesus for many miles. He will tell you it is the most exciting and fulfilling journey of his life. As you read, discuss, and practice with family and friends the habits that Greg shares, I believe you will embark on the greatest journey of your life too.

—Bob Newton

Note: Bob Newton is a Ph.D., a former missionary to the Philippines, a former seminary professor and is currently serving his fifth term as the President of the California-Nevada-Hawaii District of the Lutheran Church—Missouri Synod. But he would rather be known simply as a disciple of Jesus who is discipling others to be disciples of Jesus too. —G.F.

INTRODUCTION

FOR ORDINARY JESUS-FOLLOWERS

If you have been joining Jesus on his mission as part of your everyday life, then you can show your family and friends how to do the same. In fact, it's important that you do. And this book will help.

Believe it or not, showing your family and friends how to join Jesus on his mission is how he intends for you to participate in his Great Commission. "Showing them how" is a big part of what the gospels mean by "making disciples." Where did I get that idea? From Jesus in the gospels. If we go back there and watch Jesus, we will see that he first invites people to follow him so that he can show them how to participate in his Father's mission, and then sends them to show others how to do the same (see Matthew 4:19 and Matthew 28:19-20).

And that's how Jesus still disciples people today. He shows us how to join him on his mission as a daily lifestyle, and then he sends us to show others how to do the same. Why not start with your family and friends?

Joining Jesus—Show Me How has two parts. The first part takes you back to the gospels so that you can watch Jesus and clarify in your mind how he disciples his followers. The second part helps you leverage your newfound clarity in order to craft a simple discipling plan you can use to disciple your kids, willing neighbors or friends or fellow church members.

And do you know what will be most surprising about reading this book? (Spoiler alert!) You will feel *relief.* You will feel *hope.* You will slap your forehead and say, "Well, for heaven's sake, I can do *this.*" Turns out, discipling the way Jesus does in the gospels is much *less* complicated (and much *more* fun) than the way most of us have been raised to think about it. So this "discipling" book really is written for you. It is written for parents, grandparents, small group leaders or anyone else who wants to help their family or friends be followers of Jesus and join him on his mission too.

My wife, Susan, and I lead a ministry we call Dwelling 1:14 (www. dwelling114.org). The name comes from John 1:14: "The Word became flesh and made his dwelling among us." We come alongside Christians who are ready to gain clarity and simplicity about two things: how to join Jesus on his mission as part of their everyday lives, and how to disciple more people to do the same.

Joining Jesus—Show Me How is actually Book 2 of a two-book set that together lay out the basic content of our Dwelling 1:14 trainings on mission and discipling. If you haven't read the first book, *Joining Jesus on His Mission: How to be an Everyday Missionary,* let me suggest it. In it we help people discover the mindset, practices and support they need to join Jesus on his mission every day in the places they already live, work and go to school. It has already helped tens of thousands of people get off the bench and into the adventure of seeking the kingdom and joining Jesus. (An executive summary of that book's main points can be found at the end of this introduction.)

So the first book is about how to join Jesus and participate in his redemptive mission for the good of the people around us. This book is about how to disciple our family and friends the way Jesus does in the gospels so they can participate too.

Think about it—why aren't the 2.2 billion Christians scattered throughout the world and our local communities unleashing an overwhelming blessing on the people around them every day? *Because they haven't been discipled to.* They've been told to. They've been gifted to. But they haven't been *trained* to. Discipling is the missing link. Christians already have the gifts this broken world needs so badly; now it's time to disciple them to use those gifts for the good of others.

And you can start with a few of your family and friends. You can do this. We can help. What's the first step? Let's go see what Jesus has to show us in the gospels!

AND A NOTE FOR CHURCH PROFESSIONALS AND CONGREGATIONAL LEADERS

To my fellow leaders, we all dream about seeing a discipling movement emerge from our congregations. Disciples who make disciples who make disciples who make disciples...

Joining Jesus—Show Me How is about how to launch such a movement because it is about how to disciple people the way Jesus does in the gospels. In other words, when we start discipling people *the way Jesus does in the gospels*, a discipling movement will be the result. Having said that, this book intentionally does not address several organizational questions related to how we set up a *system* of discipleship for our congregation. And it's important that it doesn't. Here's why:

You can't develop an effective system for discipling a whole congregation until you have experience effectively discipling an individual person.

As someone once said, "In the end, disciples are not mass produced. They are handmade." However, just because disciples are handmade doesn't mean we can't expect to see lots of disciples being made through our congregations. It just means that we will first need lots of disciple-makers who know how to disciple individual people. And this book will help you get there. But the process starts with us as leaders gaining personal experience in discipling real people.

So let's begin there. Read this book and then for the next few months gather a couple of people who are willing to be discipled by you. Take them through the book *Joining Jesus on His Mission*. Follow the Discipling Plan in chapter sixteen of this book. See what you find out about discipling real people in real time as they engage real life with Jesus.

In the end, if we want to see a mission and discipling movement emerge from our congregations, we don't need to improvise new ways of discipling people. We simply need to imitate Jesus' way. He knows how it's done. He's the original architect. We just stopped following his plan as closely as he intended. So before we move ahead, let's go back and follow Jesus around in the gospels so he can show us how he disciples his followers to be everyday missionaries... who disciple everyday missionaries who disciple everyday missionaries who disciple everyday missionaries...

JOINING JESUS ON HIS MISSION: EXECUTIVE SUMMARY

STEP 1: MISSION MINDSET

Jesus is pursuing his Father's mission to redeem and restore all things.

And he invites us to join him. We don't go *for* Jesus. We go *with* Jesus. We aren't Jesus-salespersons. We are Jesus-followers. We aren't pushy and presumptuous. We are watching and listening for where his grace can be applied and a little good can be offered.

STEP 2: MISSION PRACTICES

Joining Jesus on his mission is as simple as enjoying the people around us, investing in a couple of pre-Christian friends and then seeking, recognizing and responding to what Jesus is already up to in their lives. We get into position for this by putting the 5 Mission Practices into play every day:

1. Seeking the Kingdom

2. Hearing from Jesus

3. Talking with People

4. Doing Good

5. Ministering through Prayer

STEP 3: MISSIONAL COMMUNITY

We support one another as we learn to take up this missionary lifestyle by gathering regularly with our missionary friends to share our stories of how we are joining Jesus on his mission in daily life. We use the 5 Questions as a prompt for reflecting, recognizing and sharing our stories. We do this for the encouragement, insight and accountability we need to head back into our lives and join Jesus for another week. Engaging in Missional Community can be as simple as gathering with a few interested friends in our home and using the 5 Questions, or using the 5 Questions as part of our family's dinner conversation, or taking

10 minutes at the beginning of our next church meeting to share our stories.

The 5 Questions with their corresponding 5 Practices:

1. Seeking the Kingdom: How did you see Jesus at work this week?

2. Hearing from Jesus: What has Jesus been teaching you in his Word?

3. Talking with People: What kind of conversations are you having with pre-Christians?

4. Doing Good: What good were we able to do (or could we do) around here?

5. Ministering through Prayer: How can we help you in prayer?

STEP 4: A MISSION TRIP TO OUR NEIGHBORHOOD

We intentionally enjoy and invest in the people with whom we live, work and play. We call this "neighboring." Over time, we get to know them, share stories and see what Jesus might be up to in their lives. For "neighboring" ideas, see chapter eighteen of *Joining Jesus on His Mission*.

CONCLUSION

We don't try to change our whole congregation. We change our own mindset and practices and invite a few friends to come along for the adventure. If we embrace the mindset and practices above, we will gain real mission experience and see real mission results.

JOINING
JESUS
SHOW ME HOW

How to Disciple
Everyday Missionaries

PART I

Regaining Clarity and Simplicity for How Jesus Disciples His Followers in the Gospels

CHAPTER 1
WHY DOES THE INVITATION TO DISCIPLE PEOPLE SCARE US?

"Let not your heart be troubled."

—*Jesus in John 14:1*

"Go and make disciples."

These words of Jesus inspire us, but they also scare us. In fact, they scare us almost as much as when he says to us, "You will be my witnesses." And wouldn't you know it, being his witnesses and making disciples are two of the main things Jesus gives us to do.

Great.

So as you pick up this book on how to disciple people, are you already pretty nervous? You are not alone. As I travel the country, I find *most* Christians get pretty nervous when the subject turns to discipling others. I hear things like: "I can't do that! I don't know enough!" Or, "I'm not spiritual enough. That's *way* too important to leave to me!" We desperately want to delegate discipling to someone who knows more about it than we do. We have a complicated understanding of discipling that leaves us feeling like it is best left to the professionals.

The very idea of discipling our own children, or a couple of friends, or a new believer is *scary* to us.

On the other hand, what if I told you our fear of discipling comes from our *mis*understanding of what discipling is? What if I told you the way we attempt to disciple people in these modern days with classes and curriculum bears little resemblance to how Jesus disciples his followers in the gospels? Somehow, over the generations, a myth has grown up around discipling. We have come to believe that discipling is so complex, so scholarly, so beyond the ability of simple Christians that only biblical scholars and spiritual superheroes should attempt it.

But this myth stands in sharp contrast to what we see Jesus actually doing in the gospels. The way Jesus disciples people must be simple because it results in unschooled, ordinary followers discipling others to be followers too. We see the evidence of this throughout the book of Acts as Christianity spreads rapidly. Our trouble? We seem to have lost track of how Jesus discipled his followers in the gospels. We need someone to show us how again.

But who? Truth be told, even pastors and church professionals aren't too sure about how to disciple people the way Jesus does. No one showed them how either. In fact, more and more pastors and church professionals are convinced that while they are well educated they are under-discipled. I received a note from a young pastor that sums this up well:

> "I would enjoy speaking to you about ways I can start discipling as a leader. I was struck by your comment during your presentation about how we use up so much energy trying to get the whole church to change instead of focusing on the people who are listening and willing to be discipled. I have realized my energy was so centered on changing the WHOLE church (which is just

crazy) that I wasn't discipling those who are willing. So the big question now is *what do I do*? I am realizing that I have been in church all my life but have never really been discipled as a Christian before. So now that I am a pastor myself, I find myself stuck with a desire to disciple my people but little training in how to do it."

See what I mean? He needs someone to show him how too. Looks like we're all in this together. Parents and pastors, church leaders and small-group facilitators. Does that mean we are stuck? Not even close. What it does mean is that we all get to start in the same place:

- at the beginning;
- in the gospels;
- with Jesus;
- learning the ABCs of discipling from him.

Before Jesus gives anyone his Great Commission to make disciples, he gives his Great Invitation to *be* discipled. "Come, follow me. Let me show you how." Are you game?

As I said earlier, my wife, Susan, and I lead a ministry we call Dwelling 1:14. We come alongside Christians who are ready to gain clarity and simplicity about two things: how to join Jesus on his mission as part of their everyday lives, and how to disciple more people to do the same. The process of regaining such clarity and simplicity can seem hard at first because we literally have to rethink *everything*. But the result is a mission and discipling plan that is clear, simple and *doable*.

For Susan and me, the journey to clarity and simplicity began by asking some specific questions about mission and discipling:

- What is the mission of God according to God?

- How does he intend for us to participate in his mission?

- What is a disciple according to Jesus?

- What does a disciple do according to Jesus?

- How does Jesus disciple people?

- What is Jesus' discipling curriculum and classroom?

As we tried to answer these questions, we began to realize that we didn't know nearly as much as we thought about mission and discipling. The answers we did have were more like presumptions—and they were generally unclear and complicated to boot. We presumed that "Of course we know what mission and discipling is!" But the more we dug into the gospels, and the more we compared our way with Jesus' way, the more our presumptions unraveled. We started to see how thoroughly our understanding of mission and discipling had been shaped not by what Jesus actually did in the gospels but by what the church had done over the last few centuries. So we decided to approach the questions solely in light of what Jesus had already told us and shown us in the gospels.

It was like pulling the proverbial thread and seeing the whole sweater unravel. It changed everything.

In light of how Jesus engages mission and discipling in the gospels, our whole paradigm shifted from:

- complex to simple;

- classroom to relationship;

- academic to experiential;

- and a process that requires a religious professional to a process where everyone gets to play

As we wrestled with what Jesus had already said and done in the gospels, we had a whole series of what we now call "blinding flashes of the obvious." It took a lot of unlearning, reexamining, experimenting and making mistakes, but we discovered that the answers we sought about mission and discipling had been in the gospels all along. Jesus had already been showing us. We just hadn't recognized what we were looking at.

So now we'd like to save you some time and streamline your pathway to clarity by sharing our hard-won "blinding flashes of the obvious" with you. Our goal is to help you regain the clarity and simplicity of how Jesus disciples people in the gospels so that you can disciple your children, friends, neighbors or fellow church members to join Jesus on his mission too. And the best part? You don't have to take our word for it. You can go back to the gospels and verify everything for yourself.

As we will see, Jesus disciples people in the gospels by inviting them to join him on his mission. When Jesus says, "Come, follow me," it is an invitation to be discipled, but the *way* Jesus disciples them is *by joining him on his mission*. So if you have been joining Jesus on his mission in everyday life, believe it or not, you are better equipped than you thought to start discipling people the way Jesus does.

Hmmm... seem too simple? Consider that, somehow, Jesus started with a handful of unschooled, ordinary disciples (Acts 4:13) who, within three hundred years, multiplied to millions. Consider that, somehow, millions of disciples knew what to do—they engaged in self-sacrificing service with joy, faced persecution with peace and spread the Good News of God as a lifestyle (see Acts 8:1-4 for an example). Why are we not seeing these kinds of discipling results in our part of the world today? Could it be that we have lost track of the clarity and intentionality Jesus had as he discipled his followers in the gospels? Could it be that we have made something intended to be simple and clear into something unclear and complicated? Have we inadvertently substituted a system of prolonged scholarship for Jesus' process of intentional discipleship? Have we turned simple "good news" into a long stream of "correct doctrinal statements"? And could it be that our resulting fear and desire to delegate discipling to professionals has stalled Jesus' movement among us in North America?

If so, let's return to Jesus and begin imitating his way of discipling again. We don't have to make up something new. We don't have to go to a seminary and learn something hard. Turns out, discipling the way Jesus does in the gospels is less about mastering something complicated than it is about one person showing another person what it looks like to seek the kingdom of God in real life and participate in his redemptive mission for the good of others.

"Come, follow me. Let me show you how."

Imagine parents discipling their children not only to be churchgoers on Sunday, but to be Jesus-followers on Monday. Imagine Christian friends connecting in community not only to study God's Word, but to help disciple each other to live out that Word as the aroma of Christ for their nonbelieving friends. Imagine youth volunteers not only teaching teens to live morally in an immoral culture but discipling teens to live redemptively in a culture that needs redemption so badly. Imagine lifelong members of churches discipling young believers and new believers to seek the kingdom in their daily lives. Imagine people heading out of church refreshed and ready to spend another week discipling their families, willing neighbors and interested coworkers to live life with Jesus every day.

This is not a pipedream for a few biblical scholars and spiritual superheroes. This is God's original dream for everyday followers like us. We just lost track of how to do it. So let not your heart be troubled. Turns out, discipling isn't so scary when we set aside our *mis*understandings. All we have to do is heed Jesus' invitation to "Come, follow me," and let him show us how.

Interested? Then let's go! His "blinding flashes of the obvious" await us.

HERE'S THE POINT

The goal of this book is to help you regain the clarity and simplicity of how Jesus disciples people in the gospels so that you can disciple your children, friends, neighbors or fellow church members to join Jesus on his mission too.

CHAPTER 2
WHAT IS "DISCIPLING" ACCORDING TO JESUS?

"If anyone would come after me..."
—Jesus in Matthew 16:24

I f we're going to understand what *discipling* is according to Jesus, let's start with gaining clarity on what the word *discipling* means.

Perhaps you are familiar with these words: Apprentice. Trainee. Intern. Padawan (for you Star Wars fans).

What do these words have in common? They are familiar nouns used to describe a person in the process of becoming skilled at something—like a profession, a craft or being a Jedi Knight, for example. They are also synonyms for a less familiar noun: *disciple*. A disciple is a person in the process of becoming skilled at something too. And then there are these familiar words: Coaching. Training. Mentoring. Drilling. These are verbs we use to describe the actual *process* through which certain skills are developed. As in, "The employee receives *coaching* to develop her job skills." These familiar verbs are synonyms for a less familiar verb: *discipling*. Discipling is also a process through which certain skills are developed.

So when you hear the term *disciple* of Jesus, think *apprentice, trainee, intern or Padawan* of Jesus. Likewise, when you hear that Jesus is *discipling* us, think Jesus is *coaching, training, drilling or mentoring* us.

Now the next question is, "To what end?" If a *disciple* is a person in the process of becoming skilled at something and *discipling* is the process through which the skills are developed, then what are the skills? And what are we to do with them? In other words, to what end are we being *discipled*? For that answer, we will first go to Jesus and watch how he disciples his followers in the gospels. After we have done that, we will start distilling what we have found into clear and simple summary statements. And *why* is it important to keep our understanding of mission and discipling clear and simple?

You've heard of the iPhone? On January 9, 2007, Steve Jobs took the stage at the annual Apple gathering in San Francisco. He was excited. He was about to introduce the first iPhone to the world. He knew it was a game changer. For the first time, technicians at Apple had engineered a way to combine the functions of a phone, emailing, texting and surfing the net into one handheld device. Steve Jobs held up one iPhone that day. Ten years later, there are an estimated two billion iPhones and other smartphones worldwide.

How could something so technologically complex spread so rapidly around the world? How could something only a handful of engineers fully understand be used by a six year old? Here's how: The team at Apple worked hard to clarify and simplify the technical complexities so that the *way* the phone worked was clear and simple for ordinary people. They made the iPhone so clear and simple to use, almost *anyone* could use it. And as a result, *because* it is so clear and simple to use, almost anyone can then show others how to use it too.

Here's a blinding flash of the obvious: Clear and simple spreads. Unclear and complex does not.

The goal of Apple was not to produce a product so complex that only a few iPhone *engineers* could use it. The goal of Apple was to produce a product so simple that millions upon millions of iPhone *users* could use it. Does Apple need some engineers who understand all the technological details? Of course! They are constantly looking for the brightest and smartest to continue educating and training for this purpose. But it would have been foolish for Apple to expect that every user of the iPhone would first have to be educated as an engineer in order to use it. That would have reduced their sales from billions to a trickle.

That's why we need to keep mission and discipling clear and simple too. Clear and simple spreads. Unclear and complex does not. The goal of Jesus is not to have a mission and discipling process that is so complex only a small number of theological experts can participate. His goal is to unleash a mission and discipling movement in which *billions* of ordinary followers from every nation can participate. Do we need some experts who understand all the theological details? Of course. We are constantly looking for the brightest and smartest to be our pastors and professors. But it is unnecessary to expect every ordinary follower to become a theological expert before engaging in Jesus' mission and discipling movement. That would reduce what should be a worldwide movement down to a trickle.

Remember, iPhones are designed for *lots* of ordinary iPhone users. Likewise, Jesus designs mission and discipling so that *lots* of ordinary followers can participate with him too.

So back to our original question: What exactly is "discipling" according to Jesus in the gospels? Albert Einstein once said, "If you can't explain it simply, you don't understand it well enough." Sounds like a worthy goal. So over the years, I have settled on the following summary: discipling is Jesus' process of showing the people of God how to participate in the mission of God as a daily lifestyle. Let me say it again: discipling is Jesus' process of showing the people of God how to participate in the mission of God as a daily lifestyle. Could it be that simple?

Well, let's go find Jesus in Matthew 4 and find out. Matthew 4 is one of the places in the gospels where we see Jesus initiating his discipling process with people. He approaches two brothers and says in verse 19, "Come, follow me, and I will make you fishers of men." Jesus is on a mission. He has been sent by his Father to redeem and restore all things. When Jesus says, "Come, follow me," he is inviting the brothers into a training process so they (the people of God) will be able to participate in the mission of God as a daily lifestyle. This training process then continues to unfold throughout the rest of the Gospel narrative until Matthew 28, when Jesus commissions them to make even more disciples who will participate in the mission of God too.

But it starts here in Matthew 4:19, where we quickly learn four things about Jesus' discipling process:

1. Being a disciple of Jesus starts with Jesus.

    Jesus initiates the discipling process and it is born from his grace. He comes to them. He chooses them and befriends them. He gives them a new identity and a new vocation. And then he begins to train them. "Come, follow me, and I will make you fishers of men."

2. Discipling is a process of training that changes us for the good of others.

Jesus invites them to follow him in order to train them and change them. But this change is not primarily for the good of the disciples themselves. Jesus changes them *for the good of others*. When Jesus says, "Come, follow me, and I will make you fishers of men," he is saying, "Come, follow me, and I will change who you are and what you do for the good of others."

The rest of the New Testament uses a variety of terms that are essentially synonymous with the personal change that discipling causes: Discipling = training = growing = maturing = transforming = sanctifying = conforming = being "taught to obey everything I have commanded." And all for the good of others.

3. *The way* Jesus disciples them is *through* joining him on his mission.

   Joining the mission is both what Jesus trains them *for* and *the way* Jesus trains them. Being discipled isn't something that *precedes* joining the mission. It is something that happens as a *result* of joining the mission.

4. Discipling the way Jesus does in the gospels results in disciples who make even more disciples.

   Multiplication is built into Jesus' discipling process from the beginning. In Matthew 4:19 when he invites the brothers to be discipled, he already knows his goal: to commission them to make even more disciples as he does in Matthew 28:19-20. So from Matthew 4 to Matthew 28, Jesus is showing them how to participate in the mission of God as a daily lifestyle so that they can then show others how to do the same. The way Jesus disciples his followers results in disciples who make even more disciples—who will make even more disciples—who will make even more disciples—until the nations will be discipled to participate in the mission of God throughout the entire earth. (Pretty cool, huh?) In many nations this is already happening. If we clarify, simplify and imitate Jesus' discipling process, we will see it too.

Is that what you thought discipling was? This may not be the answer you thought you'd get, but it is the answer Jesus has been giving from the beginning.

What about catechesis and catechisms? What about all the nuances and details of pure doctrine? What about the next volume of theological textbooks we still need to tackle?

I hear you. But what about, "Come, follow me"?

When Jesus disciples someone in the gospels, he says, "Come, follow me." When we disciple someone, we say, "Go to a class." Hmm... Something is off. Is this one of the reasons we are not seeing the kind of results that Jesus saw in the gospels? Is it because our understanding of discipling is not the same as Jesus' understanding? "Come, follow me" is not the same as "Go to a class."

Have we unintentionally begun substituting a system of scholarship for Jesus' process of discipleship? Have we made knowing answers *about* Jesus more important than actually *joining* Jesus in the community? Have we made "being a disciple" only for the smart kids who can master theology? There is nothing wrong with being smart or mastering theology. The problem comes when we *substitute* mastering theology for actually joining Jesus on his redemptive mission as a daily lifestyle. C. S. Lewis once observed, "Being a great theologian can easily be mistaken for being a good Christian."

Of course, studying the Word of God and discussing its theology was a key part of Jesus' discipling process. (More on this in chapter eleven, "What is Jesus' Discipling Process?") Whether as a 12-year-old boy in the Temple or in Caesarea Philippi with his disciples, he encouraged theological discussion to be rich and deep and wide ranging. But here's the question: To what end would he have us study and discuss? So we can *know* more? Or so we can *be* more and *do* more with him in our communities that need it so badly?

If scholarship is the goal of discipleship, then we end up with scholars who make more scholars who know right answers. If joining Jesus is the goal of discipleship, then we end up with disciples who make more disciples who participate in the redemption and restoration of all things. Scholarship is fine. But redemption and restoration of all things is the goal.

"Come, follow me," Jesus says. "Let me show you how to participate in my Father's redemptive mission." According to Jesus, that's what discipling is.

HERE'S THE POINT

What is discipling? According to what we see Jesus doing in the gospels, discipling is the process of showing the people of God how to participate in the mission of God as a daily lifestyle. This may not be the answer we thought we'd get, but it is the answer Jesus has been giving from the beginning.

CHAPTER 3
WHAT IS THE MISSION
OF GOD?

"Behold, I make all things new!"
—*God on his throne, Revelation 21:5 (KJV)*

To be completely accurate, discipling isn't actually the point.

That may sound odd in a book about discipling. But discipling is a means, not an end. It is a process that needs a point. So what's the point?

The point is the mission of God.

The mission of God is the unifying theme of Scripture. It's what the Bible is about. It's the one main thing. It's what God was up to in the Old Testament. It's what God was up to in the New Testament. It's what God is up to right now in little and large ways. God has a mission. And his mission is what gives purpose and priority to every other teaching and practice in the Bible. So if we don't know what the mission of God is, we are in danger of missing his point.

Susan and I were in Alaska recently and had the opportunity to talk with some bush pilots. Because there are so few roads in Alaska, bush planes are as common there as pickup trucks are in Texas. We enjoyed hearing the pilots' stories, but one conversation really stuck with us. One of the pilots told us that when you fly through the Alaskan wilderness, keeping an eye on your compass is critical. Getting lost is easy in the wide-open spaces. He illustrated his point by saying that flying even one degree off course can be disastrous. If you fly one degree off course at 60 miles per hour for one hour you will end up one mile off course. You'll miss your goal by a mile!

When it comes to discipling people, it's easy to veer off course too. It doesn't take much to veer off just a degree or two and end up missing our goal by a mile. We end up with churchgoers rather than Jesus-followers. We end up with people who know the right answers *about* Jesus but have few stories of life *with* Jesus. We end up with scholars but not missionaries. We need to keep our eye on the compass. We need to be clear about where we are heading with the discipling of our children, friends or fellow church members.

So, where are we heading? What's the point? The best place to go for that answer, of course, is God. Whatever God says is the point, is the point. And God says the point is *to redeem and restore all things through Jesus.*

"He that sat upon the throne said, 'Behold, I make all things new!'" Revelation 21:5 (KJV).

That's the mission of God. Everything else, *everything*, is a means to that end. Who says so? God.

- "And now the LORD says, 'It is too small a thing for you [Jesus] to be my servant to restore the tribes of Jacob. I will also make you a light for the Gentiles, that my salvation may reach to the ends of the earth'" (Isaiah 49:6).

- "For God so loved the world that he gave his one and only Son, that whoever believes in him shall not perish but have eternal life" (John 3:16).

- "For God was pleased to have all his fullness dwell in [Jesus], and through him to reconcile to himself all things by making peace through his blood, shed on the cross" (Colossians 1:19-20).

God wants his world back. God wants all things made new, the ends of the earth saved, all things reconciled to himself. This is the mission of God. This is the point. Everything else is a means to that mission. *Everything.* The cross and empty tomb of Jesus are means to that mission. The Word and sacraments are means to that mission. Discipling is a means to that mission. Our churches and worship services and programming are means to that mission. And so are we. The mission of God is what we are made for and saved for.

It's interesting, but though Christians are pretty specific about confessing what we are saved *from*, we're not always as specific about confessing what we are saved *for*. We confess Jesus died on the cross and rose again to save us *from* sin, death and the devil. But what are we saved *for*?

In order to understand what we are saved for all we have to do is remember what we were made for.

In the very beginning of the Bible (Genesis 1 and 2), when God starts making human beings, he tells us why he is making us. Do you remember the reason? To glorify God? To be loved by God? Nope. God is certainly glorified as we fulfill our purpose day by day. And God certainly does love us. But that's not *why* he made us. He clears up the mystery in Genesis 1:26-28: "Then God said, 'Let us make man in our image, in our likeness, and let them rule over the fish of the sea and the birds of the air, over the livestock, over all the earth...'"

God, who is invisible and intangible, had just created a visible, tangible world. How does an invisible, intangible God get his "hands" on the visible, tangible world he has just created? God's answer? Human beings. "Let us make man in our image... and let them rule over" what I have just created.

When God says, "Let us make man in our image," he isn't saying we will *look* like him but that we will *be* like him in limited, finite ways. We, of course, are not God, but we were made by God so that he could live in us and live through us in the tangible, visible world he created. God made human beings to be a unique hybrid of his created world and his own Spirit. We are made of both. In Genesis 2, it says, "... the Lord God formed the man from the dust of the ground and breathed into his nostrils the breath of life, and the man became a living being." God made human beings in such a way that we would be his finite creatures filled with his infinite character. God is infinite love, truth and goodness. Human beings are finite and limited. However, because the Spirit of God lives in us, we are filled with his love, truth and goodness while living in the created world.

Wow. So what does God want human beings to *do*?

Genesis 1 explains: "So God created man in his own image, in the image of God he created him; male and female he created them. God blessed them and said to them, 'Be fruitful and increase in number; fill the earth and subdue it. Rule over the fish of the sea and the birds of the air and over every living creature that moves on the ground.'" In relationship with God, and with the Spirit of God living in us, we are commissioned by him to fill the earth in order to rule over it as his stewards. Now, because we are currently fallen sinners who live in 21st-century America, it's easy for us to miss what "rule over" meant in the pre-fallen world of Genesis 1 and 2. Does "rule over" mean we are to dominate the created world, impose our will on it and fully exploit it for our purposes? Not even close. Jesus explains in Matthew 20:25 what "rule over" looks like in the kingdom of God: "You know that the rulers of the Gentiles lord it over them, and their high officials exercise authority over them. Not so with you. Instead, whoever wants to become great among you must be your servant... just as the Son of Man did not come to be served, but to serve, and to give his life as a ransom for many."

So we rule by serving? Yep. God made human beings to be a physical, finite expression of himself—his love, his wisdom, his goodness, his service—living in the physical world he created. He then sent us out to fill this created world in order to serve it and care for it with the physical expressions of his love, wisdom and goodness. Or as Jesus put it in Matthew 10:8, "Freely you have received, freely give." From God, through us, into the created world—this is how we "rule." It is the same way God rules over us—not as a tyrant who is all about himself, but as a servant who is all about others. This is what God made us for. Pretty cool setup, huh?

It lasted exactly three chapters.

By Genesis 3 human beings throw it all away. Instead of being a means by which God's love, goodness and care are spread throughout the earth, we become a means by which sin, ruin and death are spread. Romans 5:12 explains it this way: "Just as sin entered the world through one man, and death through sin, and in this way death came to all men, because all sinned..." you get the idea. Thanks to us, God's cool setup has become a ruined mess.

But God so loved the world that he wouldn't let sin, death and the power of the devil prevail. God formed a new Adam, named him Jesus and sent him into the world to launch the rescue mission that would get his world back.

The first part of the plan was to save human beings *from* sin, death and the devil. Jesus did that through his life, death and resurrection. Check.

- "For just as through the disobedience of [Adam] the many were made sinners, so also through the obedience of [Jesus] the many will be made righteous" (Romans 5:19).

- "For he rescued us from the dominion of darkness and brought us into the kingdom of the Son he loves, in whom we have redemption, the forgiveness of sins" (Colossians 1:13-14).

The second part of the plan was to breathe his Spirit back into us so we could again be sent out to take up our original role in the created world. Remember what happened the evening of Jesus' resurrection in John 20:21? "Again Jesus said, 'Peace be with you! As the Father has sent me, I am sending you.' And with that he breathed on them and said, 'Receive the Holy Spirit.'" Doesn't that sound like Genesis 1 and 2 again? "And [the Lord God] breathed into his nostrils the breath of life, and the man became a living being" (Genesis 2:7).

So with sin, death and the devil taken out of us and the Spirit of God breathed back into us, Jesus can recommission us to take up the role we were made for and now are saved for. Instead of spreading ruin in the created world, we are back to spreading his love, goodness, service and truth... like we were made to do in the first place. From God, through us, and into the world that needs it so badly.

To what end? That all things be made new. That all things be reconciled to the kingdom of the Father. That all things be redeemed and restored. That's the point. That's the mission of God. Jesus didn't save us so we could sit on the bench and run out the clock until we die and go to heaven. He saved us for getting off the bench and joining him on his redemptive mission every day.

And then to show our children, friends and fellow church members how to do the same.

HERE'S THE POINT

The mission of God is to redeem and restore all things to himself through Jesus. And we get to help. It's what we were made for and saved for. Discipling, then, is the means for showing the people of God how to participate in the mission of God as a daily lifestyle.

(For a practical exploration of how to join Jesus on his mission see my first book, Joining Jesus on His Mission. *An executive summary of that book's main points can be found at the end of the introduction.)*

CHAPTER 4
MY SMALL PART IN GOD'S GREAT BIG MISSION

"After all is said and done, more is said than done."

—*Aesop*

As I talk with people across the country, I find that one of the biggest reasons why people shrink back from getting up and getting started with joining Jesus on his mission is that the mission itself seems overwhelming.

And it is.

After all, the mission of God is *global* in its scope. It is by definition *massive*. It includes *every* person in *every* community in *every* nation. As I write this, there are approximately 7.2 billion people spread out over 57.3 million square miles of the face of the earth. How in the world can our small lives make a difference when the mission of God is so enormous?

Unfortunately, one of the main casualties of feeling overwhelmed is that we start to feel the concrete mission of God morph into an abstract idea. The mission is no longer something we do; it is something we talk about... at church... in sermons and meetings. Its scope is simply too much. Thus, what Aesop observed about humans long ago still applies to mission today: "After all is said and done, more is said than done."

Well, hold on there. Before we give up, let's do some math. You see, while there are 7.2 billion people on the face of the earth, 2.2 billion of them are baptized Christians. That leaves five billion unbaptized people. Still overwhelming, right? But if we do the math, do you know how many unbaptized people there are per Christian on earth? Not millions or thousands or even dozens. There are two.

Five billion unbaptized people divided by 2.2 billion baptized people is roughly two people each. Millions or thousands or even dozens would be overwhelming. Two is not. Two is doable. Looks like Jesus' overwhelming mission isn't so overwhelming after all. All that needs to happen is for each of us to take up our very small part of his great big mission.

You see, the *scope* of God's mission is, indeed, global. It is as massive and expansive as the earth and everyone on it. But the *focus* of God's mission is radically local and radically personal. We don't start with the whole earth. We start with our nearest unbaptized neighbor or friend. We can't win the *world* for Christ until we meet our *neighbor* who needs Christ. So, what's their name? What's their story? As simple as it sounds, getting to know and offering friendship to one or two of them is how we engage the massive, global mission of God. And if each of the 2.2 billion Christians on the face of the earth took up their small part? Wow...

Imagine 2.2 billion Christians taking the next year and starting to get to know and offer friendship to one or two of the unbaptized people nearby? What if we stopped being overwhelmed by the 4,999,999,998 unbaptized people who we don't know and started to invest in the one or two who are already nearby? The magazine *Christianity Today* recently reported that in the U.S. 20% of unchristian people don't know even one Christian personally. Is it because no Christians live nearby or work alongside them? Is it because no Christians hang out at the same coffeehouses or brew houses? Is it because no Christians work out at the same gym or have kids in the same school? Hmm...

But this could change. And easily.

What if all the people in church worshipping Jesus this Sunday went home and did the one thing Jesus gave us to do? What if all the people in church worshipping Jesus this Sunday went home and started loving their neighbor as themselves? Not the nations, not the city, not thousands or hundreds, just the few already nearby.

Of course our first response might be, "But I don't want to." Understandable. But if that is our response, then we are in danger of missing the point. You see, this isn't about what we want to do. This is about what Jesus *disciples* us to do. Baptized and trained Jesus-followers love their neighbors. This is who we are. This is what we do. We are Jesus-followers and we join Jesus on his redemptive mission.

By the way, mission is much easier and a lot more fun when we get to know our neighbor's name and a little of their story. Fred Rogers, from *Mr. Rogers' Neighborhood*, used to say, "It's hard not to like someone once you know their story." Are you tempted to dislike your neighbor, judge your neighbor or avoid your neighbor because they are so... whatever you disapprove of? Then draw deeply from the grace God offers you, and invite that neighbor over for a meal. During your time together, have the goal of getting to know a little of their story. Then replace your neighbor in the story with yourself. What would you be like if you had grown up in the environment they had? What would you be like if you had been caught in the consequences of one or two of your bad choices like they had? What would you be like if what had happened to them had happened to you? And if you had ended up "that way," wouldn't it be a blessing from God to have a neighbor nearby who treated you with the kind of love you didn't deserve but needed so badly? Wouldn't it be a blessing from God to have a neighbor who took time to get to know you and really listen to you? Wouldn't it be a blessing to have a neighbor nearby who wasn't repelled and judgmental like a Pharisee but patient and redemptive like Jesus?

This is who we are. This is what we do. We aren't given the job of fixing our neighbor or saving our neighbor. Our job is much simpler. We are to love our neighbor, as the Father has already loved us. This is our small part of his great big mission.

If 2.2 billion of us each took up our very small part, his great big mission would come to pass.

So far in this chapter we have focused on unbaptized people. But perhaps your heart has also been aching for a loved one who is baptized but has walked away from Jesus. You may be wondering, "Don't they count too?" Of course they do... and dearly. The point of our math illustration isn't to dismiss anyone. The point is to help us realize the mission of God is *doable*. So let's say a full 50% of the 2.2 billion baptized people in the world have walked away. That's 1.1 billion people! However, once again, math helps. How many "baptized-but-gone" people are there for each of the 1.1 billion baptized people who remain? One. If each of us would take up our very small part, the great big mission of God would come to pass. (In my book *Joining Jesus on His Mission*, I refer to people who are either unbaptized or have walked away from Jesus as "pre-Christians.")

Theologians have a word for this idea of "taking up our very small part of God's great big mission." The word is "vocation." The word "vocation" means "calling" and comes from the Latin word *vocare*. The teaching of vocation highlights that every Christian is called by God to particular people, particular places and particular opportunities. We are not called to *everywhere* but to *somewhere*. We are not called to *everyone* but to *someone*. God gives us a specific vocation in order to focus us and aim us for daily life. He saves us from being overwhelmed and stymied by all the options and potentials out there. God gives us specific people to love and influence, specific places to dwell in as his tangible presence and specific opportunities to seek and fulfill with him.

If we wonder, "Where in the world should I join Jesus on his mission?" or, "What should I do?" He responds with, "How about starting where I have already put you and doing what I have already dropped in your lap to do." That's vocation.

Each of us is uniquely and wonderfully made and each of us has a unique and wonderful life situation into which God has called us. So where has God already put you? Where do you live, work, play, work out, hang out or go to school? And who are the people who already live with you, live near you, work alongside you or go to the same school as you? What are their names? What are their stories? This is your vocation. This is your calling. Not to millions of places and billions of people, but to the few already within reach.

Acts 17:26 reminds us, "God determined the exact places where they should live." Do you sometimes wonder *what was he thinking*? We already know what he was thinking: that, for now, you would join him on his mission as he redeems and restores these neighbors and this neighborhood, these coworkers and this workplace, these classmates and this school.

So don't be overwhelmed by the mission of God; let yourself be impressed. It's a great big mission, but he has broken it down into little local parts for each of us: two or three pre-Christian friends where we already live, work and play.

Now that's doable.

HERE'S THE POINT

We are not called to join Jesus on his mission in millions of places among billions of people. Instead God gives us a very small part of his great big mission. There are only two or three pre-Christian people for every Christian on earth. Not thousands or dozens. Two or three. Our small part begins with simply getting to know and offering friendship to a couple pre-Christian people whom God has already put nearby. And then see what he does from there!

CHAPTER 5
ARE WE UNDER-DISCIPLED
FOR THE MISSION OF GOD?

"A long obedience in the same direction..."
—Eugene Peterson

My dog is named Pippy and she sits really well.

Unfortunately that's all Pippy does really well. It's not her fault. She's not a bad dog or a dumb dog. She is an undertrained dog. I should know because I accidently undertrained her. I didn't do it on purpose. It's just that I don't know much about training dogs.

I *intended* to train her to do more than come to me and sit. But the one thing we actually work on is her coming to me and sitting. So that's what she does really well. I'm pretty sure she could have been trained to be a very good hunter and fetcher. I have seen the instincts in her as we are out for our walks. I see her instincts for searching and finding. She has the instincts but not the training.

She is now nine years old. The other day I threw a ball past her and said, "Fetch!" She looked at me, a bit bewildered, as if to say, "That was weird. What is 'fetch'? I really have no idea what you're talking about." She didn't get it. And why should she? I never trained her to know what "fetch" might mean or how to do it.

On the other hand, "Sit!" she gets and does very well.

Eugene Peterson, a pastor and author, has a phrase about discipling I have come to appreciate. He refers to discipling as "a long obedience in the same direction." In other words, the kind of disciple we are becoming is a result of what we do or don't do habitually over time. Discipling is not a result of what happens in any one day but of what happens day after day.

With my story of Pippy, if I change the word from "training" to "discipling," we have a pretty good illustration of what Eugene Peterson means. Pippy is really good at coming to me and sitting because that is what she is "discipled" to do every day. It is our habit. It is her "long obedience in the same direction." We don't spend any time at all on finding and fetching. No wonder she thinks I'm weird for throwing a ball past her and shouting, "Fetch!" As far as fetching is concerned, she is under-discipled.

In the same way, if you're like most churchgoing Christians, you have mostly been discipled to come to church and sit. "Coming and sitting" is our "long obedience in the same direction." We come and sit in worship. We come and sit in classes. We come and sit in meetings. So as followers of Jesus, it's what we do really well. On the other hand, we show signs of being under-discipled in some other important areas of following Jesus. For instance, going home from church and joining Jesus on his mission in our daily lives.

Imagine if one Sunday your pastor suddenly switched from "Come to church" to "Go and join Jesus." Many of your fellow church members might look just as bewildered as Pippy did when I told her to "Fetch!" And why wouldn't they? They haven't been discipled to join Jesus on his mission in their daily lives. They've heard about it in sermons, studied it in Bible classes and talked about it in committee meetings.

But they've not been *discipled* in it. There's been no long obedience in *that* direction.

It can be very frustrating to realize we are under-discipled. After all, we did what we were told to do by our pastors and parents! We went to church and Sunday School every Sunday. We volunteered to lead committees and teach classes. We became respected for our theological knowledge. Having said that, we nevertheless *feel* under-discipled when we think about following Jesus into the mission field of our own community. We feel under-discipled when we think about "seeking first the kingdom of God" outside of church services. We feel under-discipled when we realize that Jesus didn't tell us to delegate disciple-making to pastors but to disciple our children, friends and neighbors ourselves.

Indeed, realizing that we are under-discipled can be frustrating, but it can also be catalytic. It can propel us to ask new questions and seek Jesus' answers:

- Do I know how to seek the kingdom of God in the midst of my busy life?

- Do I know how to join Jesus on his mission?

- Is my sweet spot as a Jesus-follower at church on Sunday or am I also ready to roll with him on Monday?

- Do I know how to disciple others to do the same?

If the answer to these questions is "Not yet," then it is time to start a long obedience in a *new* direction—the direction Jesus set a long time ago.

Now are you wondering, "Wait! What about my church?! Doesn't going to church have a part to play in discipling me?" Of course it does. The question is *what* part it plays. Worship is a means. Word and sacraments are means. Studying the Bible is a means. Fellowship is a means. To what end? Enabling the people of God to participate in the mission of God as a daily lifestyle.

Do you enjoy watching football? If so, do you turn on the TV or buy a ticket because you are excited to watch your team huddle? Of course not. That's not the point. You're not watching the game to see your team huddle. You're watching the game to see your team score and win! That's the point. You know huddling is important. The team needs some time to take a breather and call the next play. But you also know your team can't score from the huddle. The huddle is a means to an end. At some point the team needs to break the huddle, go to the line of scrimmage and run the play.

In the same way, Christians often forget that while huddling with one another at church is important, it's not the point. It's important, but it's a means not an end. We need Word and Sacrament, we need encouragement, we need insight, we need one another. But in the end, the point of all our huddling is to head to the line of scrimmage and run the play. And the play Jesus calls time after time is the mission of God. Sadly, what often happens is that we forget to actually go run the play. We break our huddle and say, "See you next week!"

Instead, as your family heads home after church, ask this question: "How will this [service, class, activity] help us join Jesus on his mission this week?" The question helps us remember that the point of the service, class or activity is to help us run Jesus' play. The question can also help church leaders keep church huddles properly focused on being a means for helping the people of God participate in the mission of God as a daily lifestyle.

Now, let's get back to our main question: if we are currently under-discipled when it comes to important priorities like joining Jesus on his mission and discipling others to do the same, how can we get more fully discipled by Jesus? That's simple. We do what every other person did in the gospels who wanted to be discipled by Jesus: we get up and actually join him on his mission.

Here's how it works: Remember that being a disciple of Jesus starts with Jesus. He comes to us. He calls us. He initiates. In the gospels Jesus comes to Peter and Andrew as they cast a net. Jesus comes to James and John in their boat. Jesus comes to Matthew at the tax collector's booth. Jesus comes to them personally to start the discipling process. And how does Jesus come to us these days to start the discipling process? In Matthew 28:19 Jesus says it is through baptism. "Go and make disciples... baptizing them..." Jesus comes to each of us personally through our baptism. According to Jesus, this is the first step in making us into his disciples.

Why baptism?

In Romans 6:3 Paul explains that it is because we are baptized *into* Christ Jesus. Paul is saying that baptism is the way by which Christ Jesus comes to live inside of us. Baptism isn't some kind of religious ritual. God breathing his Spirit into Adam wasn't a ritual. It was the way by which his Spirit literally came to live inside of Adam and Adam became a living being. In the same way, we are baptized *into* Christ Jesus so that Christ Jesus literally comes to live inside of us and we become alive in him. Being baptized *into* Christ = Christ coming *into* us. And because he now lives inside of us, he changes who we are and what we have. He changes our identity. We are now forgiven and restored to our proper relationship with the Father and our intended purpose in his created world.

- "I have been crucified with Christ and I no longer live but Christ lives *in* me. The life I live in the body, I live by faith in the Son of God, who loved me and gave himself for me" (Galatians 2:20).

- "Or don't you know that all of us who were baptized into Christ Jesus were baptized into his death? We were therefore buried with him through baptism into death in order that, just as Christ was raised from the dead through the glory of the Father, *we too may live a new life*" (Romans 6:3-4).

- "For we are God's workmanship, *created in Christ Jesus to do good works*, which God prepared in advance for us to do" (Ephesians 2:10).

For Peter, Andrew, James, John and Matthew their discipling started with Jesus coming to them. And according to Jesus, our discipling starts with his coming to us too, through baptism. However, though discipling starts through baptism, it is not completed. In order for us to continue being discipled by Jesus, there is the next step: getting up and actually joining him on his mission. In other words, it's time to let Jesus train us. (This is why Jesus pairs baptism in Matthew 28:19 with training in Matthew 28:20.)

Think about Matthew the tax collector. He is sitting at his booth in Matthew 9:9 doing what he does. Jesus comes up to his booth and says two words: "Follow me." Jesus comes to Matthew, forgives Matthew and invites him to get up and be discipled.

But what if Matthew had stayed seated? What if he had said, "Thank you, Jesus!" but then did not get up from his tax collector's booth and actually follow? Would he still have been loved by Jesus, forgiven by Jesus, wanted by Jesus? Of course! That's why it's called grace. But Matthew wouldn't have been *discipled* by Jesus. Matthew wasn't going to experience a life changed by the *training* of Jesus if he stayed seated at his booth. That would only happen for Matthew when daylight appeared between his britches and the bench.

And that's exactly what happened. "Matthew got up and followed him" (Matthew 9:9). That's when Matthew's training began. That's when Matthew began figuring out what it meant to live on mission with Jesus. To sum it up, three things came into play when Matthew got up and actually joined Jesus:

1. Matthew was being discipled by Jesus (trained, changed, shaped, taught, grown);

2. people around Matthew were blessed as he lived his life like Jesus;

3. and Matthew was gaining experience he would later use to disciple others to do the same.

Perhaps this explains some things about us too. Have we been baptized but remained seated at our booth? Have we thanked Jesus for his salvation but then declined his training? If so, what are we missing out on? What parts of our heart and life are left unaffected and under-discipled? Or have we, like Matthew, gotten up and joined Jesus on his mission? Are we gaining more experience week by week? Do we have new stories to tell about life on mission with him?

These may seem like hard questions, but they can help us gain clarity about how discipling works—or about what's been missing. If getting up and actually joining Jesus on his mission has been missing for you, he has good news. It's never too late for you to start. His invitation to be discipled still stands. He says, "Repent, believe the good news and follow me. But this time," he adds with a smile, "let me see some daylight between your britches and the bench."

HERE'S THE POINT

If we are currently under-discipled when it comes to important priorities like joining Jesus on his mission and discipling others to do the same, how can we get more fully discipled by him? That's simple. We do what every other person did in the gospels who wanted to be discipled by Jesus: we get up and actually join him on his mission.

CHAPTER 6
THE RUB RESOLVED: HOW JESUS CHANGES US THROUGH DISCIPLING

"You are in me, and I am in you."

—Jesus in John 14:20

Here's the rub.

It's a wonderful thought that we would get to participate in the mission of God. But to be honest, for our participation to be redemptive and restorative for others, we need to be a lot less like our natural selves and a lot more like Jesus. The math is simple. Same old me = same old results. That means it's not pretty for others. Same old me = impatience, anger, selfish motives, barbed comments. Ouch and yuck. On the other hand, me becoming more like Jesus = me having more love, joy, peace and patience for others. Me becoming more like Jesus = others getting blessed.

And there's the rub. I can't get there on my own. I'm stuck. Same old me = same old results. As someone once observed, "What got you here won't get you there." The good news is that Jesus comes to change the math. He changes the equation: Same old me + Jesus + his discipling = new me blessing others. Jesus resolves the rub by intervening on my behalf and discipling me. He changes who I am and trains me to be more like him for the good of others. How does this work? Let's find out by unpacking two questions.

1. According to Jesus, what does "becoming like him" look like?

2. How does Jesus enable us to become like him?

So what does "becoming like Jesus" look like? There is no mystery there. According to Jesus, becoming like him means having an increasing capacity to love others. In John 13:35 Jesus says, "By this all men will know that you are my disciples, if you love one another." Pretty straightforward. The evidence that a person has been discipled by Jesus is not her knowledge of theology, or attention to keeping rules, or time spent at church. The evidence is her increasing capacity for loving others. And the rest of the New Testament builds on that simple truth.

- Galatians 5:22, "But the fruit of the Spirit is love..." (In other words, the evidence that the Spirit of God is inside of you is the love of God coming out of you.)

- 1 John 4:7-8, "Dear friends, let us love one another, for love comes from God. Everyone who loves has been born of God and knows God. Whoever does not love does not know God, because God is love."

- Galatians 5:6, "For in Christ Jesus neither circumcision nor uncircumcision has any value. The only thing that counts is faith expressing itself through love."

- 1 Corinthians 13:1-2, "If I speak in the tongues of men and of angels, but have not love, I am only a resounding gong or a clanging cymbal. If I have the gift of prophecy and can fathom all mysteries and all knowledge, and if I have a faith that can move mountains, but have not love, I am nothing."

According to Jesus, "becoming like him" looks like serving others with love. But Jesus does not characterize this love as a sappy love given only to the loveable. The love he speaks of and gives is a gritty love. It is a redemptive, restorative love that does its best work in the midst of anger, hatred, ruin and opposition. In a word, it is grace. Grace is not loving the loveable. Grace is loving the unlovable. Grace is treating people better than they deserve. God treats us better than we deserve and he calls us to do the same for our neighbor. It's the world's only hope.

So becoming like Jesus looks like grace. It looks like self-sacrificing service for the good of others—and especially for those who don't deserve it. Rats.

- Matthew 16:24, "If anyone would come after me, he must deny himself and take up his cross and follow me." (In other words, if we want to consider ourselves to be disciples of Jesus, we must give our lives for the good of others like he does. Rats.)

- Luke 6:32-35, "If you love those who love you, what credit is that to you? Even 'sinners' love those who love them... But love your enemies, do good to them, and lend to them without expecting to get anything back." (Rats.)

- Matthew 20:26-28, "Instead, whoever wants to become great among you must be your servant... just as the Son of Man did not come to be served, but to serve, and give his life as a ransom for many." (Rats.)

- John 13:14-15, "Now that I, your Lord and Teacher, have washed your feet, you also should wash one another's feet. I have set you an example that you should do as I have done for you." (Rats.)

And there's the rub. This is all *well* beyond us. If that's what "becoming like Jesus" looks like, we are done. We simply don't have it in us.

Exactly. That's why we need Jesus. He changes the math and enables us to become like him: same old me + Jesus + his discipling = new me blessing others. Jesus resolves the rub by intervening on our behalf and discipling us. He changes who we are and trains us to be more like him for the good of others. Here's how he does it.

First, as we saw in the last chapter, Jesus literally comes *into* us through baptism (Romans 6:3). Through baptism Jesus changes who we are and what we have. He replaces our old self with himself. He replaces our sin with his Spirit. In John 14:20 Jesus says, "On that day you will realize that I am in my Father, and you are in me, and I am in you." Baptism is simply the way this becomes a reality for each of us personally. "You are in me, and I am in you." *This is who you really are.*

Wow.

Because Jesus is in us through baptism, we now have what it takes in us to love the unlovable and offer grace to the undeserving. It's pretty simple: "Love comes from God" (1 John 4:7). From God, through us, to the undeserving. If you're reading this and wondering, "Where in the world does this kind of love come from?" The answer is, "From God." You already have his abundant love. So, "Freely you have received, freely give." You don't have to wonder whether you have it or enough of it. You don't have to chase after it or earn it. You can simply remember that you already have it. And then offer it to the next person who needs it so badly. This was all settled when you were baptized.

What the Father said of Jesus at his baptism he said of you at yours: "This is my son (This is my daughter) whom I love; with him (with her) I am well pleased."

Now, do you know what happens when you actually believe that—when you believe you are loved by the Father? Joy starts to bubble up in you. You already have an abundance of joy in you because you are baptized into Christ, but it wasn't bubbling up as long as you forgot that you are loved. But when you remember you are loved, here comes joy! And on the heels of joy, do you now see what is emerging? Peace. Love and joy together call forth peace. And with love, joy and peace, look what now is within reach... patience. You already had it as a gift. It's been yours since you were baptized into Christ. You just forgot that you are loved by the Father, so it seemed far away. But remembering you are loved jump-starts the chain reaction toward patience. After that, look what starts tumbling forth... kindness, goodness, faithfulness, gentleness... and finally even self-control emerges not as an effort of our own but as a fruit of his Spirit and love.

So through baptism we now have Jesus in us, which changes who we are and what we have at our disposal every day. Jesus says, "Have no fear, little flock, for your Father has been pleased to give you the kingdom" (Luke 12:32).

Q: Who am I in Christ?

A: I am a beloved child of the Heavenly King.

Q: What do I have in Christ?

A: The things of his kingdom and in abundance.

This is who we are. This is what we have.

This restoration of our true identity in Christ is the first part of how Jesus resolves our rub. The Bible calls it our *justification*. It is the realm of gift and grace. Justification is the Holy Spirit's work *without* our participation. It is simply given to us. However, now that our true identity in Christ has been restored, *what do we do*? We join Jesus on his mission and he trains us to live like him in a world that needs it so badly. This is the second part of how Jesus resolves our rub. The Bible calls it our *sanctification*. This is the Holy Spirit's work too, but it is *through* our participation. It is the realm of effort, practice and training. Jesus makes this clear when he says, "*Follow me*, and I will make you to become..." (Mark 1:17 ESV). Jesus is saying that he will be the one making us into what we will become, but it will be *through* our participation. And it will require our hard work.

Taken together, justification and sanctification are the two parts of discipling. Discipling *starts* for us through baptism (Matthew 28:19). But discipling is not *completed* through baptism (Matthew 28:20). There is now the training, maturing and hard work that happens as we follow Jesus and learn his lifestyle. This is the "teaching them to obey everything I have commanded you" part of the discipling process. What Jesus gives as a gift in baptism he matures through the hard work of training.

That was another blinding flash of the obvious for Susan and me: what baptism gives, training now matures.

It is like the person born with the gift of a healthy body who then needs to train it in order to excel as an athlete. The body is a gift given without her participation, but becoming an athlete requires her participation in training and hard work. It is like the person born with the gift of a healthy mind who then needs to train it in order to become a top student. The mind is a gift given without his participation, but becoming a top student requires his participation in training and hard work. The same is true for the child of God. We are reborn through baptism with the gift of a restored identity in Christ. It is a gift given without our participation. But becoming a disciple who is on mission for the good of others requires our participation in training and hard work with Jesus.

This hard work with Jesus matures us, humbles us and teaches us to obey so we become more and more like him in how we live. Becoming more like Jesus certainly is not about seeking to attain some kind of earthly perfection like Jesus has. It is simply participating in the mission of God as forgiven sinners in our limited, finite ways. But don't miss it: These limited, finite ways look like Jesus to the world. Love given—even imperfectly—looks like Jesus. Service offered—even imperfectly—looks like Jesus. A little grace humbly extended—instead of what is deserved—looks like Jesus. Jesus calls us to participation not perfection.

Our daughter Ellen is currently a senior at a public high school with 2,500+ students. She was baptized within days of her birth. Jesus restored her true identity nearly 18 years ago. She has been in training *with* Jesus ever since. For most of her years in elementary school, middle school and now high school she has been in a large setting with many, many kids who have not yet received the grace and truth of Jesus. They are smart, talented and insightful kids. But many are also hurting, confused and at risk. Susan and I could have tried to avoid this kind of exposure for Ellen. However, the truth is, every school—parochial, private or public—has kids who need the grace and truth of Jesus. So we see each day as an opportunity for Ellen to be discipled as she joins Jesus on his mission to kids who need him so badly. Sometimes it has been easy and fun for her, and sometimes it has been excruciating. But, oh, how she has grown! Jesus is training her to be redemptive by being with people who need redemption. And her capacity for treating others with his grace and serving others in humility has increased considerably over the years. She exhibits the character of Jesus so much more than I did at her age. But then again, she has so much more training too. Her baptism *gave* her Jesus; her training has helped her become more *like* Jesus for the sake of her classmates and friends.

Rub resolved. Thank you, Jesus.

HERE'S THE POINT

To become redemptive in the world with Jesus we need to become more loving like Jesus. And there's the rub. Jesus resolves the rub for us through baptism and training. He restores us to the abundant love of the Father through baptism and then he trains us to give away that love to those who need it so badly. "Freely you have received, freely give."

CHAPTER 7
WHAT IS MY DISCIPLING PLAN?

"Is that what Jesus told you guys to do?"
—An atheist named Matt Casper after attending church

So what's your discipling plan? Before you attempt to disciple your family and friends, it would be good to have a plan, right?

In my first book, *Joining Jesus on His Mission*, we unpacked how we can join him on his mission in the places we already live, work and go to school. Now how do we turn and disciple *the next person* to join Jesus too? What's the process? If someone wanted to learn how to be a follower of Jesus—your child, a friend at work or a fellow church member—what would you do?

Before you answer, let me tell you a story.

Have you ever been to a Pizza Ranch? I live near Houston, Texas. And around here we don't have Pizza Ranch restaurants. But in the upper Midwest they are a *big deal.* A few years ago I was in Sioux Falls, South Dakota, as part of my work with Dwelling 1:14. A pastor and I had been talking on the phone during the previous months making plans for initiating a missional discipleship process in his congregation. It was now time for me to come to town and start working with the leaders directly. I was arriving in Sioux Falls on a Friday night. And, well, if you wanted to show someone a good time in Sioux Falls on a Friday night, the place to go was the Pizza Ranch. So I met them there.

When I arrived at the Pizza Ranch, the parking lot was packed. I knew the pastor and could see him standing with a group of people near the front door of the restaurant. I parked and went over to them. We made our introductions and stepped to the front door. Because I was the guest of honor, I was ushered to the front of the group. Someone opened the door for me. I thanked them, stepped inside and... froze. It was chaos in there! There were buffet lines weaving in every direction and people flowing in and out of them with some kind of instinctive understanding of what one does when one eats at the Pizza Ranch.

The problem? I was not one of those people.

So I stood frozen in the doorway, not knowing what to do. How did someone get started in there? Where was I supposed to go? The dessert line was right by the front door. Philosophically I liked the idea of starting with dessert, but I was pretty sure it didn't work that way!

Of course this took all of three seconds to buzz through my head, even though it felt much longer. Thankfully, someone I had just met outside stepped in beside me. His name was Jay. Jay had clearly been to the Pizza Ranch before. And Jay did something that immediately lowered my anxiety level and got me moving in the right direction. You know what he did?

He handed me a 43-page training workbook explaining how to enjoy your first meal at the Pizza Ranch. He then escorted me to a side room where first-time customers could enroll in a six-week class using the workbook.

No, he didn't. Instead Jay offered two words that lowered my anxiety level and got me on my way to enjoying my meal. Know what he said?

"Follow me."

It wasn't a booklet. It wasn't a class. It was a new friend with a simple plan. "Follow me so I can show you how to get started." Turns out, Jay's simple plan worked really well. Jay could have had a complicated plan. He could have tried to teach me everything there was to know about the Pizza Ranch before taking me inside to eat. He could have required me to understand how to use the kitchen equipment, recite pizza recipes and have a working knowledge of the employee handbook. It could have taken weeks. It could have taken a workbook. And that would have been fine. But it would have been a really long time before I got to eat any pizza from the buffet line. Instead Jay chose a simple plan. "Follow me." He showed me some things, and pointed out some things, and in short order I was eating pizza like a veteran Pizza Ranch guy.

Jay's plan was simple. And so is the plan of Jesus.

Jesus is on a mission, and we get to help. But in order for us to be helpful, Jesus needs to disciple us. And his plan is a simple one: on-the-job training. He says, "I know you don't know what you're doing yet. So come with me. Let me show you how to participate in my Father's mission." In other words, by having us participate with him on his mission, he trains us for his mission. Simple. Brilliant. (Of course it would be. It's Jesus' plan.)

As we consider what our discipling plan will be, doesn't it make sense to imitate Jesus' plan? In fact, that *is* the plan. In Matthew 28, having discipled his followers, Jesus then commissions them to disciple even more people. But he doesn't tell them to make up a *new* plan for discipling people. He tells them to imitate *his* plan. Jesus essentially says, "In the same way as I have discipled you, go and disciple others, until the nations are discipled in my ways." Simple. Brilliant. (Of course.)

Well, his plan may be simple, but getting our heads around it *seems* hard because it is so different from our prior experience and expectations. It is so... *simple*... it requires a paradigm shift in our brain. (Ouch!)

And here comes our next blinding flash of the obvious: The way Jesus disciples people in the gospels looks more like an invitation to pursue a friendship than it does an invitation to pursue a course of study. It feels more like a series of conversations with a friend than it does a series of lectures in a classroom. As simple as it sounds, one of the biggest keys for discipling the way Jesus does in the gospels is *being with the people you are discipling and spending unhurried time together.*

- Mark 3:14, "[Jesus] appointed twelve... that they might be with him..."

- Luke 8:1, "Jesus traveled about from one town and village to another... The twelve were with him, and also some women who had been cured..."

- Acts 4:13, "When they saw the courage of Peter and John and realized that they were unschooled, ordinary men, they were astonished and they took note that these men had been with Jesus."

Even his invitation to "Come, follow me" is, at its core, an invitation to be with Jesus. In other words, being discipled *by* Jesus means being *with* Jesus. This is not just a passing detail but a key part of his discipling plan.

So what does discipling look like?

It looks like a relationship. It looks like a conversation about how life is going and how Jesus might be involved. It looks like a man I know who spends time on Saturdays showing a neighbor's grandson how to work on the lawn. The grandson is a teenager who came to live with his grandpa because he got in trouble back home. The grandpa asked my friend if he had any odd jobs his grandson could do. He offered to let the teen do his yard, but the kid did a really bad job. In the process, though, my friend realized there was more at stake than a well-manicured yard. So he started working *with* the kid. He spent time with him, showing him how to do the work, how to repair the equipment... and they talked. They talked about little stuff at first, but over time, bigger stuff too. And now they talk about life stuff. And Jesus. This is what discipling looks like: intentional time together, unhurried conversation about real life and Jesus—and the kingdom comes.

Discipling looks like the conversations we have around our dinner table at night or at breakfast in the morning. Whether with our own children or the young adults we sometimes host, there is a lot of laughter, good questions and listening to one another's stories. And along the way, we get to show them things and point out things about life and life with Jesus. This is what discipling looks like: intentional time together, unhurried conversation about real life and Jesus—and the kingdom comes.

Discipling looks like a friendship I recently heard about. A Christian author and speaker named Rosaria Butterfield tells the story of how God led her to faith in Jesus through an unlikely friendship with a pastor and his wife. Before becoming a Christian, Rosaria was a PhD who taught in the English department of Syracuse University. She was an atheist, had adopted a lesbian identity, and was an activist for

LGBTQ issues. Through an interesting set of circumstances, she was introduced to a Bible-believing pastor and his wife. Rosaria expected the encounter to be confrontational and antagonistic. Instead she experienced grace. The couple invited her to have dinner at their home. Instead of confronting her and trying to convert her, the couple offered friendship and hospitality. Rosaria found that they were genuinely interested in her and her story. They asked questions and listened. They let her ask her questions and air her fears and grievances. After a few more dinners, they became friends. During their conversations, the pastor and his wife would show Rosaria Jesus. It happened naturally as they would point things out to her along the way—as they highlighted a little grace here, or explained a little truth there. They weren't in a hurry. And Rosaria met Jesus along the way. She became his follower in 1999. And she now disciples others to do the same. This is what discipling looks like: intentional time together, unhurried conversation about real life and Jesus—and the kingdom comes.

So what will be your plan for doing that?

When I work with people to help them clarify and simplify their discipling plans, I start with a self-discovery exercise. I have them sketch out a flow chart of their current discipling plan. It's usually a very revealing exercise.

There's a book I read some years ago called *Jim and Casper Go to Church*. It's a book about a Christian leader named Jim who invites an atheist friend named Matt Casper to come with him to several churches across the U.S. The goal is to participate in these congregations for a weekend and get honest feedback from Casper about what he heard and saw. After attending one of their first church events, Casper asks Jim, "Is that what Jesus told you guys to do?" He wasn't being snarky. He was genuinely perplexed. He knew enough about the teachings of Jesus to know something wasn't lining up. The organization representing Jesus didn't seem to be imitating him very closely.

"Is that what Jesus told you guys to do?" I find the question to be catalytic and clarifying.

So after people have sketched out their discipling plans, I ask them Casper's question: "Is that what Jesus told you guys to do?" As the people look at their plans, they generally see that they fall into one of three categories:

1. **No plan at all**. If a person wants to be discipled (that is, they want to learn how to be a follower of Jesus), we send him or her to the pastor to figure something out.

2. **A plan for scholarship**. In this kind of plan, discipleship is primarily about scholarship. We send the person to classes. We have Sunday School classes, confirmation classes, new member classes, Bible study classes and maybe even some "discipling" classes. We evaluate progress by asking, "Is this person learning enough?" With this kind of plan, Jesus' invitation to "Come, follow me, and I will make you fishers of men" morphs into "Come, follow me, and I will make you a scholar." Classes can be good. But what about discipling?

3. **A plan for membership**. In this kind of plan, discipleship is primarily about membership. We send the person through an assimilation process. We have lots of options for groups, ministries, circles, teams, studies and volunteer assignments. We evaluate progress by asking, "Is this person active enough in church?" With this kind of plan, Jesus' invitation to "Come, follow me, and I will make you fishers of men" morphs into

"Come, follow me, and I will make you an active member." Being an active member at church can be good. But what about discipling?

There is a fourth option: The plan of Jesus. Jesus' plan for discipleship is **a plan for relationship**. In this plan, discipleship is primarily about relationship and we evaluate progress by asking, "Is this person in a relationship with someone who is consistently showing him/her how to join Jesus on his mission as a daily lifestyle?" With this plan, Jesus' invitation to "Come, follow me, and I will make you fishers of men" doesn't morph. It is accomplished. Disciples are made.

Is there more to discipling than this? Yes, and over the next several chapters we will follow Jesus around in the gospels so he can show us more. But this is where he starts. His framework is simple. So, as we begin to consider how we might craft a plan for discipling our family and friends, let's keep it that way. And as an added bonus, if someone does eventually ask us, "Is that what Jesus told you guys to do?" we will be able to answer, "Why, yes. Yes, it is."

HERE'S THE POINT

We need a clear and simple plan for discipling our family or friends. Instead of making up our own plan, we can imitate Jesus' plan. It looks like a relationship: intentional time together, unhurried conversation about real life and Jesus—and the kingdom comes.

A QUICK WORD TO CHURCH LEADERS:

1. As you can imagine, a discipling plan that centers on relationship ends up looking very different from the plans we

currently see used in congregations. As a consequence, some leaders might be reluctant to implement such a plan because of the anticipated disruption and confusion it could cause. However, a discipleship plan centering on relationship does not need to prove disruptive if it is introduced as a next step for people who are willing and ready to be more intentionally discipled. In other words, current classes and programming can become a pathway and funnel to more intentional discipleship.

2. Likewise, as leaders evaluating your congregation's discipling plan, do not be tempted to make unnecessary "either/or" choices between scholarship, membership or relationship. Scholarship, membership and relationship goals each have significant roles to play in our congregation. We need some of each. Instead evaluate your plan and *prioritize* the goals. Ask, "How will we prioritize the congregational activities that support our scholarship, membership and relationship goals? In what will we invest our best resources first?"

CHAPTER 8

WHAT QUALIFIES ME TO DISCIPLE OTHERS?

"When you come to personal dealings with others,
remember who you are—not a special being made up
in heaven, but a sinner saved by grace."

—*Oswald Chambers*

The goal of this book is to regain the clarity and simplicity of how Jesus disciples his followers in the gospels so that you can disciple your children, friends, neighbors or fellow church members to be followers of Jesus too.

However, many Christians will not even consider discipling their family or friends because they harbor a common misunderstanding. They presume they're *unqualified* to do it. It sounds something like this: "How could I possibly disciple other people?! Look at me, I'm a mess. I don't know enough about my Bible, I'm not very spiritual, and I am painfully aware of how often I struggle with my doubts."

Are you pretty sure your imperfections should disqualify you from discipling others? Well, if perfection was a qualification, we would certainly be unqualified. But perfection doesn't even show up on Jesus' list! Neither does being super spiritual, having deep Bible knowledge or having overcome all doubt and fear.

Really? Yep.

What qualifications *do* make Jesus' list? Let's go back to Matthew 28 and Acts 1 where Jesus is launching his discipling movement and take a closer look. (You might be surprised.)

Most Christians are familiar with the words of the Great Commission: "Go, and make disciples of all nations." However, there are a couple facts you might have overlooked. For instance, do you remember how many people stood before Jesus to receive his Great Commission? In Matthew 28:16-19, we are told, "Then the eleven disciples went to Galilee, to the mountain where Jesus had told them to go. When they saw him, they worshipped him; but some doubted."

Did you catch the answer? The group is not 5,000 strong or 3,000 or even 120. It is 11. Jesus gives the Great Commission to *11* disciples. Wow. That's not very many. There are usually more people sitting in the back two pews during our church services than are standing before Jesus in this passage. And then it gets worse. The narrative goes on to say that some worshipped Jesus, "but some doubted." *Some doubted?* Unbelievable! Jesus is giving the Great Commission to people who still have doubts? I don't know about you, but I guess I always assumed Jesus gave the Great Commission to an army of strong believers who had everything figured out. I pictured them having halos on their heads, stalwart faith in their hearts and indisputable theological wisdom on their tongues. Evidently not so much.

Having laid bare these surprising imperfections, Matthew goes on to record the Great Commission itself. "All authority in heaven and on earth has been given to me," Jesus says. "Therefore go and make disciples of all nations." Clearly Jesus *wants* them to go and make more disciples since he authorizes them to do so. But it begs the question:

what *qualifies* this undersized, ragtag group of imperfect followers to disciple other people? Authorization doesn't necessarily mean qualification. I could authorize a 10-year-old to drive my car, but that doesn't mean she would be qualified.

The word "qualified" means to be officially recognized as having met the requirement for performing a particular job. So what qualifies the disciples to disciple others? Jesus gives us the answer. *It is their experience and their stories of life on mission with him.*

"You are witnesses of these things" (Luke 24:48).

Ever since Jesus called the disciples to follow him in Matthew 4:19, he had been qualifying them to make more disciples. He had been giving them on-the-job training for pursuing his Father's mission. He had built up their experiences day by day. And they had been accumulating Jesus-stories. By the time Jesus says, "Go and make disciples," these 11 disciples are no longer inexperienced novices. They are not perfect, they still have doubts and they lack many qualities. But Jesus wasn't training them to be perfect. He was training them to participate in the mission of God. And by Matthew 28, they had experienced enough to show others how to participate in the mission of God too.

We see it again in the last encounter between Jesus and his disciples in Acts 1. Jesus is about to ascend to his Father. But, of course, the disciples are still struggling. They still have doubts. They still lack answers. So the disciples ask Jesus, "Lord, are you at this time going to restore the kingdom to Israel?" (Acts 1:6). But Jesus knows they are missing the point... again. So he tells them, "It is not for you to know the times or dates the Father has set. You will receive power when the Holy Spirit comes on you; and you will be my witnesses in Jerusalem, and in all Judea and Samaria, and to the ends of the earth." In other words, don't worry about what you *don't* know. Tell people what you *do* know and the Holy Spirit will use it powerfully.

Jesus authorizes them, their stories qualify them and the Holy Spirit empowers them.

So that clears some things up for us, doesn't it? The Great Commission was given to an undersized group of unschooled, ordinary people who were imperfect, lacked theological insight, suffered from doubts but had joined Jesus on his mission. Sounds like our kind of people! So if you ever think "discipling" isn't for you because you are imperfect, lack some theology and occasionally have doubts, forget about it. You're exactly the kind of person Jesus has used and will continue to use powerfully to the end of the age.

Of course, there is *one* thing that leaves us unqualified to disciple others: *if we have not yet joined Jesus on his mission.* What the Holy Spirit used powerfully throughout the book of Acts were the disciples' stories of life on mission with Jesus. "As for us, we cannot help speaking about what we have seen and heard" (Acts 4:20). If all we have is theological book knowledge, we are not yet qualified to disciple others. If we have no experience in joining Jesus on his mission, we are not yet qualified to disciple others. Why? Because we have no stories... yet. On the other hand, if you have been joining Jesus on his mission for even a short time, you know enough to help the next person get started too. You have a few stories to tell. You can show others what you've found out. According to Jesus, that's discipling. And it's important that you start.

I boarded a plane not long ago and took my seat. It was going to be a full flight and it wasn't long before someone sat down next to me. I looked up to see a young man covered with angry tattoos. I greeted him and immediately thought to myself, "Jesus, what are you up to here?" After we had leveled off at 32,000 feet, I got out my Bible to do some reading. The young man with the angry tattoos pointed to my Bible and said something I had not expected. "Cool book." Over the next several minutes I was surprised to find out this young man with the angry tattoos was a redeemed follower of Jesus. He had indeed been very angry, and a drunk and an addict for much of his young life. But when he finally realized he needed to do something or die, someone introduced him to AA. At AA he found a humble community of people who were struggling with their own recovery but still eager to help him get started with his own. And through them he met Jesus.

As he told his story, I soon found out that one of the keys to the recovery process is having a sponsor. A sponsor is someone who has been through the 12 steps and is willing to walk alongside you throughout your recovery journey. Perhaps most surprising is that a sponsor is not someone who is "cured" of their addiction or an expert in the science of recovery. They are simply fellow alcoholics who have been working the 12 steps long enough to be able to guide others as they begin their own recovery journey. Sponsors don't know everything, but they know enough to help the next person get started. What qualifies them to be a sponsor is not their perfection at recovering but their experience in recovering. And that's true for you too, as you prepare to start discipling your family and friends.

You're not perfect and you don't know everything, but if you have been joining Jesus on his mission even for a short amount of time you know enough to help the next person get started. And it's important that you do. Your children, your interested friends, the other members of your church group *need* you to start sharing your stories of life on mission with Jesus. How else will they know? Who else can show them how?

HERE'S THE POINT

What qualifies us to make more disciples? Our experiences and stories of joining Jesus on his mission. Jesus authorizes us, our stories qualify us and the Holy Spirit empowers us.

CHAPTER 9

WHAT IS A DISCIPLE ACCORDING TO JESUS?

"It takes courage to grow up and become who you really are."

—ee cummings

A young pastor I know was having an elders meeting. He had just returned from a conference and was passionately advocating that the congregation refocus its resources on making disciples. The elders were all for it. The room quickly filled with an excitement and unity that only a worthy vision can generate. The discussion became excited as ideas and tactics were brainstormed back and forth. Then one of the elders hesitantly raised his hand and asked a simple question: "Pastor, if we're supposed to make disciples, what is one?"

Good question.

It stopped the discussion cold. They all realized that in spite of their excitement and unity, they lacked clarity. However, the question didn't kill their excitement and energy—it focused it. They realized that before they could make plans, they needed to clarify what they were going to make.

"If we're supposed to make disciples, what is one?"

When it comes to discipling our kids, friends or fellow church members, it's easy to skip the work of clarifying and defining our discipling outcome. That's hard work. It's more fun to jump straight to considering discipling tactics. "What program should we use? What activities should we plan? Who's in charge of food?"

"We're not exactly sure what a disciple is, but let's go make some!" Hmm...

I fly around the country nearly every week. Jumping to discipling tactics without first defining our discipling outcome is like me deciding which plane to take without having a specific destination in mind. For example, if I want to fly to Chicago, then I better get on a plane that is flying to Chicago. If I have no destination in mind, then any plane will do. But if I want to fly to Chicago, then that clarity narrows down the options I should consider. There are lots of fine planes going to lots of fine places. But if I need to get to Chicago, I better take the plane to Chicago. In the same way, if we aren't clear about our discipling destination, then any "discipling" study or program will do. Unfortunately for the people we are discipling, if our plan is an unclear hodgepodge of tactics, we will end up with an unclear hodgepodge of results.

So as we start to form our discipling plan, our first job is to define where we want to end up. "If we're going to make a disciple, what is one?" Of course the best place to go for that answer is the gospels. What does Jesus disciple his followers to be and do as he launches his movement in the first place? For my friend and his elders, this discipling question launched their discipling quest to rediscover the answers Jesus gave in the gospels. What about you? How would you answer the question? If you are going to make disciples of your willing family and friends, what are they going to be and do?

Let's go see what Jesus shows us in the gospels.

For the sake of clarity, let's begin by taking a peek at where we will end up. Over the years, I have found it helpful to distill what Jesus shows us in the gospels about "what a disciple is" with the following summary definition:

A disciple follows Jesus:

- in order to become *like* Jesus (through baptism *into* Jesus and training *by* Jesus);

- so that he/she can participate *with* Jesus on his mission as a daily lifestyle;

- and show others how to do the same.

So with that in mind, let's go with Jesus and collect the details.

The context of the gospels is that Jesus is pursuing his Father's mission. He has been sent by his Father on a grand adventure to redeem and restore all creation to his kingdom. And Jesus invites us to join him. But for us to be helpful to Jesus, we need to be discipled by Jesus. And in the gospels, as we have seen, Jesus begins that process by inviting people to "Follow me." So that's why we start our summary definition with "A disciple follows Jesus."

Though this is certainly accurate, it is not specific enough. Why? Because as we watch Jesus in the gospels we soon discover that *crowds* of people follow him around. And certainly not everyone who is following Jesus is a disciple of Jesus. People in the crowds have many different motives for following him. In Luke 6:12-19 we see that the crowds following Jesus are made up of three general groups:

1. There are the 12 apostles, who are disciples but are specifically chosen by Jesus to be trained to eventually lead his mission movement (Luke 6:12-16; Acts 1:20-26);

2. there are the other disciples who are being trained to participate in Jesus' mission movement and help spread it (Luke 6:17; 10:1);

3. and finally, there is everyone else in the crowds, who are the beneficiaries of Jesus' mission movement (Luke 6:17-19).

So some follow to be discipled by Jesus, but many follow to hear his teachings, or to be healed by him, or to receive more bread and fish from him or to see if he might be the political answer to the Roman occupation. We even see those who are following Jesus simply to keep an eye on him for the authorities so they can eventually take him down. All these people are following Jesus in the crowds. But it is only a specific subset of the crowds that is identified as "disciples" of Jesus. So what are we missing?

Could it be that disciples are all the people who follow Jesus in faith and *are saved*? Well, certainly in the gospels disciples have faith and are saved, but not all who have faith and are saved are identified as disciples. Lots of people who are following Jesus also put their faith in Jesus (John 8:30) and benefit from his gifts of grace (Matthew 4:23-25). The crowds are loved by Jesus, taught by Jesus, healed by Jesus, forgiven by Jesus (Matthew 9:2) and saved by Jesus (John 5:24). And yet not all these are called disciples of Jesus.

Could it be that disciples have a superior *kind* of faith compared to the crowds? Is *exemplary* faith what distinguishes someone as a disciple? Well, not really. In the gospels we find Jesus routinely scolding the disciples for having "little faith" (see Matthew 8:26, 14:31, 16:8). At different points he says that little children and even a Roman centurion are better examples of faith than are his own disciples (Matthew 18:3, 8:10). If anything, his disciples seem to struggle *more* with faith than do average followers in the crowd.

Could it be that disciples have a stalwart *commitment* to Jesus? Nope, that can't be it. In the gospels, after disciples make the commitment to cross the line and be discipled by Jesus, we still see them wrestle with crossing back and forth over that line. In John 6:60-70 we see "many of his disciples" turning back and no longer following Jesus, in Matthew 26:14-16 we watch Judas betray Jesus, and in Matthew 26:69-75 Peter denies Jesus because a servant girl questions him. Not exactly *stalwart*.

So being a disciple of Jesus isn't about being spiritually superior to the crowds or in a class above them. And yet disciples *are* different. How?

The difference is *why* they are following Jesus.

Back in the days of rabbis and disciples, everybody understood what it meant to cross the line from being an admirer of a rabbi or a student of a rabbi to being a disciple of a rabbi. You see, someone who admires a rabbi honors the rabbi. Someone who studies about a rabbi is a student of the rabbi. But according to rabbinic tradition—and what we see in the gospels—only someone who wants to become *like* a rabbi is a disciple of the rabbi.

Disciples would follow their rabbi not only to *hear* the rabbi's teaching but to *imitate* how the rabbi lived out his teaching. They followed the rabbi to become like the rabbi. That's why we see Jesus repeatedly urging his disciples not to settle for simply hearing his words but to put them into practice (Matthew 7:26; Luke 8:21, 11:28; John 13:17, 14:23). Transformation was at stake. Henri Nouwen sheds light on this when he writes, "We do not think ourselves into a new way of living as much as we live ourselves into a new way of thinking." For a rabbi, the way he evaluated his disciples' progress was to look at how they were doing putting his teaching into practice and imitating his lifestyle as their own.

This is also why Paul urges the people he is discipling "to imitate me" and to "follow my example, as I follow the example of Christ" (1 Corinthians 4:16-17, 11:1). He wants them to be reminded "of my way of life in Christ Jesus." This is rabbi-disciple talk. He writes in Philippians 3:17, "Join with others in following my example, and take note of those who live according to the pattern we gave you," and a moment later in 4:9, he reinforces that reminder with, "Whatever you have learned or received or heard from me, or seen in me—put it into practice." Paul isn't just teaching them theological concepts like a Greek scholar, he is discipling them in a way of life like a Hebrew rabbi.

Bottom line? The goal for followers of any rabbi is to *become like the rabbi*. That's why Rabbi Jesus says in Luke 6:40, "A student is not above his teacher, but everyone who is fully trained will be like his teacher."

Having said that, are you thinking it sounds pretty ridiculous to even think about trying to be *like Jesus*? Maybe you're thinking, "How in the world can I be like Jesus?! I am just a poor miserable sinner!" Well, you see, that's the thing. No, you're not. You are not *just* a poor miserable sinner. At least not any more. You *were* nothing more than a poor miserable sinner... until Jesus got ahold of you. Now you are a forgiven sinner, a baptized sinner, a sinner who has the Spirit of Jesus living inside of you. Jesus says, "You are in me and I am in you." And Paul reminds us, "...for it is God who works *in you* to will and to act according to his good purpose" (Philippians 2:13). So because it is Jesus himself living in us, *of course* we can now live like Jesus because it is Jesus doing the living *through* us (see Galatians 2:20). From Jesus, through us, into the tangible world that needs it so badly.

It is also important to remember that Jesus is not saying we can *be* him, he is saying we can be *like* him. Remember what we saw in Genesis 1 and 2? We were not created to *be* God but to be *like* God in limited, finite ways for the good of others. The way God's unlimited, infinite love and service gets into the world that needs it so badly is through limited, finite human beings like us. And that's what we are being trained to do.

But this training does not come easily.

Back in the days of rabbis and disciples, becoming a disciple of a rabbi required a step-change in lifestyle. Becoming a disciple wasn't about signing up for a class *about* the rabbi but living life *with* the rabbi. And this was especially true for becoming a disciple of Rabbi Jesus of Nazareth. It was a costly decision. And people knew it. "If anyone would come after me, he must deny himself, take up his cross and follow me" (Matthew 16:24). Becoming a disciple of Rabbi Jesus meant you left your nets, your father, your tax booth, your earthly treasures, your*self.* A person had to consider the cost of crossing the line from occasionally following Rabbi Jesus as a hobby to becoming a disciple of Rabbi Jesus as a lifestyle.

In the gospels we see several examples of people who approach the line, but then hesitate (see Mark 10:21-22; Luke 9:57-62; John 19:38). In fact, there are *crowds* of people who hesitate to cross that line. The crowds loved hearing Jesus teach, they loved benefiting from his grace, but they hesitated at becoming his disciples. (Sound familiar?) Rabbi Jesus kept teaching and gracing the crowds; they needed it and he freely gave it. But if anyone wanted to become a *disciple* of Rabbi Jesus, there was still the line to cross. And the same remains true today. We are saved by grace through simple faith. Our true identity is restored through baptism. But whoever wants to be a *disciple* of Rabbi Jesus still needs to get up, deny himself and actually follow him in order to become *like* him.

So let's review: What is a disciple of Jesus? According to Jesus, a disciple is someone who follows him in order to become like him. And how does Jesus change a person into a disciple who is *like* him?

1. He claims us through baptism; and

2. he trains us through joining him on his mission.

Jesus claims us and trains us. He claims us through baptism by restoring our true identity as a beloved child of the Heavenly King and he then trains us to live out our true identity for the good of others. This is what Jesus is summing up in Matthew 28 with his Great Commission. He says baptism and training go together. What his baptism gives by grace, his training matures for action. Baptism and training are not two separate things. They are the two halves of the same thing. It's how Jesus makes a disciple.

So a disciple follows Jesus (why?):

- in order to become *like* Jesus (how?);

- through baptism *into* Jesus and training *by* Jesus.

And to what end does Jesus disciple a person?

- So that he/she can participate *with* Jesus on his mission as a daily lifestyle.

At first this may sound confusing: Jesus is discipling us *through* joining him on his mission *for the purpose of* joining him on his mission? Yes. Joining him on his mission further trains us for joining him on his mission. In other words, it is on-the-job training. The more we join

Jesus on his mission the more experienced we become at joining Jesus on his mission. Jesus disciples us *for* joining him on his mission *through* joining him on his mission.

So does that complete our definition? Almost. Jesus includes one last important aspect we should not overlook:

- Being a disciple of Jesus includes making more disciples of Jesus.

According to Jesus, we are not fully participating in the life of being a disciple until we are showing others how to do the same. Jesus follows up his invitation to be discipled (Matthew 4:19) with sending them out to make more disciples (Matthew 28:19-20). That means if we are planning to disciple our children, friends or fellow church members the way Jesus does in the gospels, we need to do the same thing. So our summary definition of "disciple" needs one last edit:

A disciple follows Jesus:

- in order to become *like* Jesus (through baptism *into* Jesus and training *by* Jesus);
- so that he/she can participate *with* Jesus on his mission as a daily lifestyle;
- and show others how to do the same.

Can it really be this simple? According to what we see in the gospels, it always has been. Let me ask you, is following Jesus a very complicated lifestyle that requires us to become Doctors of Theology or a very simple one that requires us to become like little children?

Turns out, discipling people to be followers of Jesus is less about mastering libraries of theology than it is about mastering a few simple practices for the good of others. By placing the priority on mastering simple practices, we do not undermine the importance of theology but upgrade the value of putting theology into practice. Theology is what we believe, confess *and* put into practice. It's not theology *or* practice. It's theology *for* practice. After all, isn't mission simply theology taken so seriously we actually put it into play for the good of our neighbors?

So that gives us a clear answer to the church elder's question: "What is a disciple?" We now have an outcome. We have a destination. We're boarding the plane for Chicago.

And now that we know what a disciple is, we are ready to find out what a disciple does.

HERE'S THE POINT

If we're going to join Jesus making disciples, we need to know what one is. According to Jesus in the gospels, a disciple follows Jesus:

- in order to become *like* Jesus (through baptism *into* Jesus and training *by* Jesus);

- so that he/she can participate *with* Jesus on his mission as a daily lifestyle;

- and show others how to do the same.

CHAPTER 10
WHAT DOES A DISCIPLE DO ACCORDING TO JESUS?

"Those who hear not the music think the dancers mad."

—A framed quote on my wall

Now that we know what a disciple is, we are ready to find out what Jesus trains a disciple to *do*.

Of course, Jesus gets the training process rolling with, "Come, follow me." He restores our true identity through baptism. But then, as we saw with Matthew, it is also critical for us to come with him so we can 1) watch how he lives and 2) begin *imitating* him and his practices in our daily lives for the good of others. This is how he trains us. We watch him and we imitate him. Then we practice it over and over again for the good of others. We attempt to live like our Rabbi. Perfectly? Of course not. We are imperfect, limited and humble. But don't miss this: we are starting to live like Jesus in a world that needs it so badly.

Noted USC professor and author Dallas Willard once wrote, "The greatest issue facing the world today, with all its heartbreaking needs, is whether those who are identified as 'Christians' will become disciples— students, apprentices, practitioners—of Jesus Christ, steadily learning from him how to live the life of the Kingdom of the Heavens into every corner of human existence."

Amen. So let's submit ourselves to Jesus' training for the good of our little corner of human existence. Ready to get started?

The Bible gives us three main places where we can watch Jesus and then imitate him:

1. in the gospels;

2. in daily life;

3. and in the lives of other experienced Jesus-followers.

First, we start in the gospels. We watch Jesus closely in the gospels so that we can imitate him in our daily lives for the good of others. In John 13:15 Jesus says, "I have set you an example that you should do as I have done for you."

I don't know about you, but it was a surprise when I first realized that Jesus not only expects us to watch him in the gospels but also to imitate what he is doing in our daily lives. For the first several decades of my life, as I read the gospels, I did so as a spectator. Jesus did amazing things and I watched. I would sit in the audience (so to speak) and be wowed as I watched Jesus do his thing.

Then there was a blinding flash of the obvious. Jesus didn't invite me to follow him so he could simply show off for me. Jesus invited me to follow so he could show me how to live like him in a world that needs it so badly. The point wasn't for me to be wowed by him but to watch and imitate him. True, we are not able to imitate all Jesus' signs and wonders, but don't forget that he *did* say, "I tell you the truth, anyone who has faith in me will do what I have been doing. He will do even greater things than these, because I am going to the Father" (John 14:12).

In the gospels Jesus isn't showing off for us. He's showing us how.

Now that he has restored our true identity through baptism, he's showing us how to believe, how to give of ourselves for the good of others, how to join his Father's mission and be a part of the redemption and restoration of all things! Perhaps these are the "greater things" Jesus is talking about.

Second, because we know what Jesus said and did in the gospels, we are better able to recognize and imitate him in daily life. What Jesus said and did in the gospels, he's still saying and doing today. The more familiar we are with Jesus in the gospels, the easier it will be to recognize him on the move in daily life and respond by imitating him for the good of others. (For more on how to "seek, recognize and respond" to what Jesus is up to in your everyday life, check out chapter seven of *Joining Jesus on His Mission*.)

Finally, the Bible also tells us to watch for Jesus in the lives of other experienced Jesus-followers. We are to watch their example as they follow the example of Christ and then imitate them in our daily lives:

- "Follow my example as I follow the example of Christ" (1 Corinthians 11:1).

- "Therefore I urge you *to imitate me*. For this reason I am sending to you Timothy... He will remind you of *my way of life in Christ Jesus*" (1 Corinthians 4:16-17).

- "Remember your leaders, who spoke the Word of God to you. Consider the outcome of *their way of life* and *imitate their faith*" (Hebrews 13:7).

In other words, experienced Jesus-followers are object lessons for us, showing us what it looks like to live the way Jesus does in daily life. Jesus says in Matthew 7:16, "By their fruit you will recognize them." We are to take note of their lifestyle and imitate them as part of our training. (The context for this can be our Missional Community gatherings. See more on this in chapter twelve, "Where Is Jesus' Discipling Classroom?")

I was talking on the phone the other day with a 33-year-old who was surprised when a 57-year-old coworker wanted to be discipled by her. My friend's surprise was rooted in a sense of being unqualified to disciple a woman who was older than her. Basically she was saying, "Who am I to disciple this mature person?" However, as we talked through what discipling is and how God uses us as his instruments, she started to realize that what the 57-year-old saw in her and wanted to imitate of her was actually Jesus. What she saw was Jesus. What she wanted was Jesus. And the 57-year-old recognized that my friend had more experience in living life with Jesus than she did. So she was asking to learn more. In terms of experience as a Jesus-follower, the 57-year-old was much less mature than the 33-year-old and wanted to follow her example as she followed the example of Christ. This is discipling. People watch us and want to imitate us. But it is not us they seek. It is Jesus. It is his fruit in us that they recognize and want to imitate.

So, that's *where* we are to watch for Jesus in order to imitate him: in the gospels, in daily life and in the examples of other Jesus-followers. Now, *what* is Jesus doing that he wants us to imitate?

We might presume his list is endless! When we read the gospels, doesn't it seem like Jesus is trying to juggle a thousand different practices? In reality, his list is quite focused and simple. I have found it helpful to summarize what we see Jesus doing in the gospels with what I call the 5 Lifestyle Practices of Jesus:

1.   Jesus remembers his true identity and mission: this is who he is, this is what he has, this is what he does.

2. He seeks the kingdom: he looks for the good the Father has prepared in advance for him to do.

3. He humbles himself: when he sees the good to be done (the forgiving, loving, serving, blessing, healing, teaching, dying and rising), he submits to the Father's timing and purpose in the moment. He doesn't hesitate, procrastinate or evaluate. He submits.

4. He freely gives: he offers a little of what he has already freely received in abundance from the Father—his love, joy, peace, patience, grace and truth.

5. And he shows others how to do the same.

It may seem like there are a thousand different practices swirling around Jesus in the gospels. But these are his primary practices out of which flows a simple, redemptive lifestyle. And this is what Jesus invites us to imitate.

For those of you who have read my book *Joining Jesus on His Mission: How to be an Everyday Missionary,* you may be wondering what relationship there is between the 5 Mission Practices I advocate there and the 5 Lifestyle Practices of Jesus presented above. Great question! Though they are certainly related, the two sets of practices are intended for two different applications. The 5 Mission Practices get us *ready* for joining Jesus. The 5 Lifestyle Practices help us to *imitate* Jesus. The 5 Mission Practices answer the question, "How can I be ready for whatever Jesus may be up to today?" The 5 Lifestyle Practices of Jesus are the way we actually imitate Jesus' simple, redemptive lifestyle for the good of others.

So let's unpack the 5 Lifestyle Practices of Jesus. (For more on the 5 Mission Practices, go to chapters eleven to sixteen of *Joining Jesus on*

His Mission.) Jesus' first practice is to remember his true identity and mission. Jesus knows who he is, what he has and what he is about. And he practices remembering it.

The true identity of Jesus was announced and affirmed by his Father at his baptism. All four gospels see Jesus' baptism as his starting point, the source out of which flows the rest of his life and story. This is because at Jesus' baptism all doubt about "who he is, what he has and what he is about" is taken away. The Father himself establishes Jesus' true identity: "This is my Son, whom I love; with him I am well pleased" (Matthew 3:17). Who is Jesus? The Son of the Heavenly King. What does Jesus have? The King's love and approval in abundance. What is Jesus to be about? His Father's mission. Others would call Jesus many things—some honoring to him, some not. The devil, the crowds and even Peter would try to tempt Jesus away from his primary mission. But none of that mattered to him or distracted him. Jesus knew who he was, what he had and what he was about. "I am the Son of the Heavenly King and I have his love and approval to do what he has given me to do."

And Jesus shows us how to do the same. This is the first practice Jesus is training us to imitate as part of a daily lifestyle.

This practice reminds us that what we do flows out of the abundance of who we are and what we have from the Father. Throughout the gospels, Jesus remembers his true identity and draws on it as he pursues his Father's mission. A powerful example of this practice in play is found near the culmination of Jesus' earthly ministry in John 13:3-5: "Jesus knew the Father had put all things under his power, and that he had come from God and was returning to God; so he got up... and began to wash his disciples' feet." What Jesus was doing flowed out of his remembering—remembering he is the Son of the Heavenly King, remembering where he has come from and to where he is returning, remembering he has all things under his power. "This is who I am. This is what I have. Therefore, this is what I do."

And Jesus would have us do the same.

Like Jesus, the Father sets our true identity in our baptism. We are baptized into Christ Jesus (Romans 6:3). With Jesus in us, this changes who we are and what we have. In our baptism, what the Father said of Jesus, he now says of us: "This is my Child, whom I love; with him/with her I am well pleased." And now, like Jesus, what we do can flow out of remembering who we are and what we have from the Father:

- "Have no fear, little flock, for your Father has been pleased to give you the kingdom" (Luke 12:32).

- "Freely you have received, freely give" (Matthew 10:8).

- "As I have loved you, so you must love one another" (John 13:34).

- "As the Father has sent me, I am sending you" (John 20:21).

Do you ever wake up in the morning and face your day with a crisis of confidence? Do you ever feel inadequate for the work before you? Does "overwhelmed" fit? The source of these feelings is how we have answered the question of our identity. "Who am I? I am inadequate. I am overwhelmed. I am worried and upset about many things." We've answered the question of identity with our inadequacies and what we lack. No wonder we are worried and upset.

"I am nothing. I am worthless. I am a failure. I am a mess. I am weak. I am dumb. I am awkward. I am what I look like. I am a lost cause. I am a sinner."

No, you're baptized. What defines you is not your failures or successes, your strengths or weaknesses, your addictions, mental health status, employment status, marriage status, sexual orientation, personality or looks. As Paul says in 1 Corinthians 6:11, that is what you *used* to be. What defines you *now* is that Christ is in you. What defines you *now* is that you are "washed in the name of the Lord Jesus Christ and by the Spirit of our God." What defines you *now* is that you are loved by the Father abundantly and already have his full approval— done, yours, given—because you are in Christ through baptism.

That's why Jesus' first practice is so important for us to imitate. It makes *all the difference*. We can either live on the basis of who we are on our own without Christ (cue the anxiousness) or we can remember who we are in Christ (here comes the confidence). "Who am I? I am baptized into Christ. I am washed. I am forgiven. I am a beloved child of the Heavenly King. I have the things of his kingdom in abundance. And I can do all things through him who gives me strength." That's who we really are. That's our true identity. We are "new creations." We are "God's workmanship." We are "more than conquerors." We have "life abundantly." We have "the fruit of the Spirit." We have "the love the Father has lavished on us." This is who we are. This is what we have. (See 2 Corinthians 5:17; Ephesians 2:10; Romans 8:37; John 10:10; Galatians 5:22; 1 John 3:1.)

If we have a crisis of confidence it is simply a lapse of memory. Who we really are and what we really have in Christ has not changed at all. We just forgot. We forgot our true identity. The solution is to simply remember our baptism and then remember who we truly are. Remembering is the difference between confidence and anxiousness, striving and peace, burden and joy, having trust and having to take control. Being in Christ doesn't mean we no longer have to deal with hard times or temptation. It's *how* we deal with hard times and temptation... and overcome them... with Christ.

Answering the identity question was a big deal for St. Paul too. There are 21 letters (called Epistles) in the New Testament written by Peter, John, James, Jude and Paul. The phrase "in Christ" is used 83 times in these letters. Of the 83 uses, 79 of them are by Paul. For Paul, having our identity rooted in Christ is a big deal. And he should know. Formerly, Paul's identity had been rooted "in the Law." That's who he was. He was striving, anxious, overzealous, legalistic, judgmental and self-righteous. He was opposed to grace and a persecutor of forgiveness. He was a Pharisee. That was his identity.

But God decided to change Paul's identity by putting the Spirit of Christ into him. Paul was now "in Christ." This changed not only Paul's allegiance and confession. It changed *him*. Listen to Paul in 2 Corinthians 5:17: "Therefore, if anyone is *in Christ*, he is a new creation; the old has gone, the new has come!" Suddenly Paul is given in Christ everything he had been hopelessly striving after in self-righteousness. And Paul never got over it. Paul never got over Jesus and his grace. It was his new identity. It was his new starting point, compass heading and source. And it fueled how he lived from then on.

So before all the other practices of Jesus, there is this first practice. He shows us that what we do flows out of remembering who we are and what we have in him.

Q: Who am I in Christ?

A: I am a beloved child of the Heavenly King.

Q: What do I have in Christ?

A: I have the things of his kingdom and in abundance—his love, joy, peace, patience, grace and truth.

This is who we are in Christ. This is what we have in Christ.

And what do we *do* with the abundance we have been given? That's simple. We imitate what Jesus does with it: We go out looking for people who need a little of what we already have in abundance. This is the good the Father has prepared in advance for us to do (see Ephesians 2:10). And when we see the good to be done, we submit to the Father's timing and purpose in that moment. We don't put off the Father's timing and purpose or second-guess him. Then we freely offer a little of what we already have in abundance. (And, of course, we show others how to do the same.)

As we read the gospels, these 5 Lifestyle Practices emerge as Jesus' "basic training" for the disciples. Jesus runs them through these drills over and over again. They are applied and exemplified in a thousand different ways, but over and over again Jesus models these 5 Lifestyle Practices:

- As you read the gospels, watch for how often Jesus points to his Father as the one from whom he receives his identity, love, approval and direction. (Practice #1: remember your true identity and mission.)

- Watch for how often Jesus coaches his disciples to open their eyes and keep alert for the good the Father would have them do. (Practice #2: seek the kingdom.)

- Watch for how often Jesus has to remind them—and remind them and remind them—to get over themselves. Last is first, serving is ruling, least is greatest, pride invites humiliation. If we are full of ourselves, we are of little use. But if we humble ourselves like a little child, we are ready. (Practice #3: humble yourself.)

- Watch for how often Jesus practices his own words, "Freely you have received, freely give." Out of his abundance he pours out abundance for the good of others. (Practice #4: freely give.)

- Finally, having trained them, he sends them out to show others how to participate in his mission too. (Practice #5: show others how.)

Jesus is not showing off for us in the gospels. He is showing us how. This is what he is training his disciples to do.

Paul sums it up well in Ephesians 2:8-10: "For it is by grace you have been saved, through faith—and this not from yourselves, it is the gift of God—not by works, so that no one can boast. For we are God's workmanship created in Christ Jesus to do good works, which God prepared in advance for us to do."

Why did God do all that work of grace-ing us and faith-ing us in Christ Jesus? It is so that we can again do the good that the Father has prepared in advance for us to do. *What* good is the Father's concern. The timing, sequence and purpose of it are also in the Father's hands. We're not in charge of timing. We are not in charge of sequence. We are not in charge of results.

(Repeat this to yourself three times: "I release control to the Father.")

I love the way *The Message* translation renders Romans 8:15: "This resurrection life you received from God is adventurously expectant, greeting God with a childlike, 'What's next, Papa?' God's Spirit touches our spirits and confirms who we really are."

Yes.

I have a framed quote hanging in my writing room: "Those who hear not the music think the dancers mad." I love that quote because I can, at times, seem a little odd to others. But I also love it because it is a metaphor for what it looks like to live our lives remembering our true identity in Christ. It is as if we can hear beautiful music that is just out of range for the world. It is the music of true identity. It is the music of love and approval. It is the music of abundance. And it makes us dance as we look for those who need a little of what we have in abundance. The world sees us dance and it looks like joyful service, it looks like giving generously, it looks like peace that surpasses understanding. And they wonder, "Where does this joy come from? Where does this graciousness come from? Where does this peace come from?" And they think us mad. But we're not. We are simply living out our true identity and mission.

This is who we are, this is what we have and this is what we do.

HERE'S THE POINT

Jesus wants us to watch him, imitate him and practice what he shows us over and over again for the good of others. This is how he trains us. And what does he train us to do?

- Remember our true identity and mission;
- seek the kingdom;
- submit to the Father;
- freely offer a little of what we already have in abundance;
- and show others how to do the same.

CHAPTER 11
WHAT IS JESUS' DISCIPLING PROCESS?

"Jesus replied, 'Come, and you will see.'"
—*Jesus in John 1:39*

Anyone who has lived a little of life knows there is a big difference between hearing about something conceptually and experiencing something in real life. There is a big difference between hearing about the concept of food and experiencing a delicious meal. There is a big difference between the concept of the moon and stars and experiencing them on a cloudless night. There is a big difference between the concept of love and falling into it or the concept of music and being swept away by it or the concept of joy and being overwhelmed with it.

There is the concept but then there is the experience. And in the gospels, Jesus uses both to disciple his followers.

A couple years ago, I was with 10 pastors packed into a little bungalow in the Golden Hill neighborhood near downtown San Diego. We were listening to two men named Jon and Rob tell us about moving their families into this eclectic neighborhood filled with eclectic people in order to join Jesus on his mission. Golden Hill is an interesting place. It is a historic community with beauty and blight, wealth and poverty, culture and crime. It is ethnically diverse, an area favored by artists and musicians, but is also struggling to maintain its identity as gentrification takes root. It is a community that has long prided itself on being politically progressive. In the early 1970s war protesters gathered here, labor unions flourished here and one of the first Gay Centers in the nation was opened here.

And all the people there—like people everywhere—have a longing for redemption and restoration. What they don't yet know is that all they long for is found in the grace and truth of Jesus.

So who will bring the grace and truth of Jesus into this neighborhood of Golden Hill and offer it to these eclectic neighbors? Who will show them what it can be like to live out the grace and truth of Jesus in a community? Who will live there and be the body of Christ loving, laughing and serving in that place? Jon, Rob, their wives and children all said, "We can." Our group was eager to know, "How are you doing this? How does this work? Can you teach us?"

Their reply? "Sure. Let's go for a walk."

And just like that we pivoted from the concept of mission to experiencing it.

We left the little bungalow and went for a long walk in the neighborhood. And it made all the difference. We saw how easy it was to stop along the way and check in with people, have conversations with people and listen to people. Many were already friends with Jon and Rob. (This was not the first time they had gone for a long walk in the neighborhood.) Others had no time or interest. But that was okay too. Jon, Rob and their families lived here. There would be other walks and other opportunities.

During our walk, Jon and Rob showed us how to relax and let Jesus be in charge. They showed us how to enjoy the people we met. How to be in the moment. How to not have an agenda and not be in a hurry. They showed us how to focus on what was already happening in people's lives and to realize Jesus was already at work there. In other words, the concepts Jon and Rob had told us about in the bungalow they were now showing us in the neighborhood.

A couple of hours later when we returned to their home, we sat down, grabbed a glass of iced tea and started to discuss what we had just seen and heard. The concepts from earlier in the day had come to life. We now had some experience. It categorically changed how we engaged the conversation.

When we watch how Jesus disciples his followers in the gospels, it soon becomes apparent that Jon and Rob were using his process. They first talked with us about a variety of mission concepts and practices; we then went out for a walk and tried putting the concepts and practices into play, which gave us a much clearer and deeper understanding of what we had been talking about. By the time our afternoon together was over, we were ready to head back to our respective communities and begin imitating and replicating what we had experienced. You see, Jon and Rob had been very clever. Without announcing their intention, they had organized our time together to reflect the discipling process Jesus uses in the gospels.

And what is that process Jesus uses? I find it helpful to organize it and summarize it like this:

1. **Proclamation:** Mark 1:14, "Jesus went into Galilee, proclaiming the Good News of God."

   Proclamation is spoken-truth. And in the gospels, Proclamation is first. It is how Jesus begins his discipling process. It is not all but it is first. After all, how will they know unless they hear? So Rabbi Jesus goes from village to village telling people what they have not heard. His words reveal worlds. This is what we did in the bungalow of Golden Hill. We talked. I also refer to it as the "tell me how" step. "Tell me what I need to know." This is where preaching, teaching and Bible reading fit.

2. **Imitation/Participation:** Mark 1:17, "Come, follow me."

    Rabbi Jesus continues his training process by inviting his followers to join him so they can see how he lives out his spoken-truth for the good of others. The goal is for the disciples to watch him, imitate him and then participate with him over and over again so they gain experiential knowledge. This is what was happening as we took our walk through the Golden Hill neighborhood with Jon and Rob. I also refer to it as the "show me how" step. "Show me what I need to do."

3. **Replication:** Matthew 28:19, "Therefore go and make disciples..."

    The final part of Rabbi Jesus' training process is Replication. Soon after his followers begin engaging his training process, we see Jesus sending them out to begin replicating it with others (see Luke 8:1, 9:1 and 10:1). He sends them not because they are already experts. He sends them as part of their training. Jesus wants his disciples to show others how to take up the lifestyle practices he is showing them. This is the key to multiplying his redemptive movement. I refer to it as the "show others how" step. "It's time for me to show others what I have discovered about joining Jesus."

"Proclamation, Imitation/Participation, Replication" is simply our way of organizing and summarizing the way Jesus moves a follower from spoken-truth to experiential knowledge and then on to training others to do the same. Jesus disciples his followers using all three parts. So if we want to see Jesus' discipling results, we need to follow Jesus' discipling process.

Currently, as we attempt to disciple people, we have a heavy emphasis on Proclamation but almost completely disregard Imitation and Replication. We put all our eggs in the "tell me how" basket and wonder why people rarely move from the concept of joining Jesus on his mission to the lifestyle. Proclamation is first, but it is not all. If Proclamation was sufficient for discipling people, U.S. Christians should be the most robustly discipled Christians on earth. We have more access to Proclamation here in the U.S. than in any other part of the world. We have books and classes and websites and radio programs and conferences and billboards and yard signs and bumper stickers but... people need more than "tell me how"—they also need "show me how."

"Come, and you will see" (John 1:39).

In John 1, John the Baptist had been preparing his disciples for the coming Messiah. When Jesus walked by, John said to two of his disciples, "Look, the Lamb of God!" The disciples then started following Jesus. "Turning around, Jesus saw them following and asked, 'What do you want?'" The two disciples basically said that they wanted to know more about him. In response, Jesus simply says, "Come, and you will see." He immediately begins to help them pivot from concept to experience.

My daughter Amanda recently became certified as a Montessori teacher. She and I have been surprised to discover how many discipling principles this educational method uses. Amanda shared with me the following excerpt from one of her manuals: "Think of how hatchlings learn to fly. Not by listening quietly while an adult bird explains the various properties of flight; not by being tested and ranked on their ability to memorize and recall. For birds—and for humans—learning is best when it's active, not passive. We learn to fly by flying."

Jesus has been advocating the same thing for two thousand years. We learn to participate with him on his Father's redemptive mission by participating with him on his Father's redemptive mission. Proclamation is, indeed, first. We need Jesus to tell us what we do not know. We need his words to reveal new worlds of redemption and restoration to us. We need proclamation from pulpits and podiums, because how will we know unless we hear? Proclamation is first. But it is not all. We also need someone to show us how to live out the ways of Jesus. In other words, we need Imitation/Participation. Proclamation alone is sufficient if we are talking about spreading salvation. Romans 10:17 says, "Consequently, faith comes from hearing the message." However, if we are talking about multiplying a process that trains people to live out the ways of Jesus for the good of others, we need to add Imitation/Participation. We need someone to help us pivot from concept to experience.

"Come, and you will see" (John 1:39).

The most effective way to do this is to invite inexperienced disciples to literally come along with you and participate in a kingdom-bringing activity:

- It could be a walk together through the neighborhood like I had with Jon and Rob.

- It could be an invitation to come along to a neighborhood gathering with you.

- It could be joining you to visit someone who is isolated or hurting.

- It could be sweating side by side as together you serve widows and orphans in your community.

- It could be an invitation to sit with you and your pre-Christian friend(s) as you have a conversation about life and Jesus.

- It could be... (What is your idea?)

In this way, we help inexperienced disciples pivot from concept to experience, from telling to showing, from discussing to doing, from thinking about it to participating in it. And all it takes is a little time and an invitation: "Come with me. Let me show you."

Of course we can't always be with the person we are discipling. So a simple but effective way to help people pivot from Proclamation to Imitation/Participation when we are not together is to have them read the gospels daily and then write down their answer to this question: "As a result of what I have received from Jesus in the gospels today, what is one thing he is giving me to believe or do?" Then they can pray that Jesus would help them see opportunities to put this belief or action into play. The next time you are together, ask them how it went. Have them tell you the stories. What happened, what did they find out and what do they think they might do next? (Church leaders and teachers can include this kind of question at the conclusion of every class or sermon.)

My wife, Susan, has a simple method she has used for years as she reads God's Word and disciples others to do the same. As she reads she asks God the following questions:

- Know what?

- So what?

- Now what?

In other words she is asking God, "What would you have me know from this passage? What difference would you have it make for my life? And what do you want me to do with it?" (She picked up this method from a couple different sources who may have gotten it from a book called *How to Apply the Bible* by David Veerman.) She also has trained many parents and teachers to use this method as they prepare lessons for their kids. It moves people from Proclamation to Imitation/Participation—from concept to experience.

Which then sets us up for Replication. Replication is showing others what we have found out about joining Jesus on his mission. Once we have heard the spoken-truths of Jesus (Proclamation) and have gained some experience with Jesus (Imitation/Participation), it is time to turn and help the next person discover what we have discovered (Replication).

As we disciple our children, friends or fellow church members, it is important to include Replication as soon as possible. Jesus certainly did. Discipling that ignores or delays Replication is not following the pattern of Jesus. In our old way of thinking, having newer disciples replicate with others what they are learning from church professionals would be handled with great caution and even reluctance. After all, do they know enough? Will they do it right? In the past we would have delayed trusting someone with Replication for years. We would have wanted them to master multiple levels of learning before entrusting them with this task. But that is not the way of Jesus.

In Matthew 9:9 Jesus calls Matthew the tax collector to become a disciple. By Matthew 10:1, Jesus is already sending Matthew and the other new disciples to replicate what they have been learning. Do we really think Matthew learned everything he needed to know about the kingdom of God in less than one chapter? Did the rest of the disciples already know everything they needed to know before Jesus sent them out? Of course not. But Jesus wasn't discipling them to be fully informed scholars. He was discipling them to participate in his redemptive and restorative mission.

Can you imagine the emails Jesus would have gotten from all the worried church people?

> Dear Jesus, it is hard to understand the level of irresponsibility you have shown in sending out those "disciples" of yours after such a brief amount of training. What were you thinking? What if they had made a mistake? What if they had been asked a question to which they didn't have an answer? I can't believe you would send out such inexperienced novices to do the kind of important work we usually entrust to Pharisees who have years of training.

And I can imagine Jesus sending back a reply something like this:

> Thank you for your concern. Actually, the reason I sent them out was not because I thought they knew as much as Pharisees. I sent them out to gain experience with humbling themselves and participating in the work the Father has prepared in advance for them to do. My goal is not that they become Pharisees but that they become like little children. By sending them out to replicate with others the little experience they have had with me, I accomplished two important things: they gained even more experience for the next time I send

them out (yes, I plan to do this again), and they helped a lot of people who needed a little help. Besides, I have their back. I am literally with them all the time.

If we want to see Jesus' discipling results, we need to follow Jesus' discipling process. And Jesus' process includes sending out inexperienced disciples to replicate with others what they are finding out with us—not after years of schooling and study but later that same day (or week). We send them out and then bring them back to talk things through. We send parents to show their children. We send small group participants to show their willing friends, coworkers or classmates. We send church leaders to show their ministries, groups or committees. Then we come back together to talk about how it went.

If we want to see Jesus' discipling results we need to include all three steps of Jesus' discipling process: Proclamation, Imitation/ Participation and Replication.

In order to illustrate what all three parts look like when we put them together, imagine that I am going to coach you (disciple you) to play golf.

I start by giving you a book entitled *How to Play Golf*. (This is Proclamation/tell me how.) It contains all you need to know about golf. It has all the rules of golf and stories of great golfers of the past. I tell you to go home and master its content because in a week I am going to give you a comprehensive test. So you go home and eagerly get started. You read, you memorize and you master the content of the book. The next week you come back to take my test and score 100%. Well done!

Now, do you know how to play golf?

Well, yes and no. You correctly answered every question on the test. So in that way, yes, you "know" how to play golf. The trouble, however, is that golf is not a game of correct answers. You don't play golf by answering golf questions correctly. You play golf by putting a few simple golf practices into play over and over again until the golf ball lands in the hole.

The information *about* golf is important, but it is not all. As your coach I need to move you on to the next step, which is Imitation/Participation. You need me to show you how all the information from the book comes together in a real golf swing on a real golf course. You need me to show you so that you can start imitating how I address the ball, how I hold the club and how I take a swing. Once you see it, you can imitate it and start practicing it over and over again.

At first golf may seem complicated and awkward for you. But by imitating me and practicing, you begin to get the hang of it. Soon you know how to get up on the first tee and hit a golf shot. It may not be pretty. It may not be perfect. But you are playing golf. You are no longer on the sideline. You are playing the game. And, by the way, you now know enough to help the next person get started too. Now that you know how to play golf even imperfectly, you can show others how to do the same. After all, even below-average golfers can show beginners the basics of how to play golf.

And soon, if we keep this up, where there once was only one golfer, there will be many.

HERE'S THE POINT

If we want to see Jesus' discipling results we need to follow Jesus' discipling process. In the gospels we see that Jesus' process had three basic parts: Proclamation (tell me how), Imitation/Participation (show me how) and Replication (show others how).

CHAPTER 12

WHERE IS JESUS' DISCIPLING CLASSROOM?

"Life is a classroom. So pay attention."

—*Someone who knows what they're talking about*

These days a classroom could be anywhere. With the arrival of the internet, any space can become a place of learning. I see people taking online classes in coffee shops, parks and even airports. Learning can now literally happen along life's way.

This is nothing new for God. He has been advocating the "learn along life's way" educational strategy for a very long time.

Way back in Deuteronomy 6:4-8 God gives the following instructions through Moses: "Hear, O Israel: The LORD our God, the LORD is one. Love the LORD your God with all your heart and with all your soul and with all your strength. These commandments that I give you today are to be upon your hearts. Impress them on your children." Then he goes on to tell them how to impress the children with the ways of God: "Talk about them when you sit at home and when you walk along the road, when you lie down and when you get up." It was to be along life's way.

In Matthew 4:19 Jesus advocates the same method when he says, "Come, follow me." His invitation is to learn from him along life's way.

With Jesus any space can become a place of learning and training. He may have something to show us in our morning Gospel reading; he may have some training for us to engage at the workplace; he might give us a pop quiz at the grocery store; and he may be ready to introduce us to a new challenge when we arrive back in the neighborhood. That's how he trains us. And you just never know what he may be up to. That's the adventure of being a follower of Jesus. With him our classroom is literally everywhere.

So let's pay attention.

I don't know about you, but for decades I missed this. I used to presume that discipling only happened in a classroom with the Word of God and an experienced teacher. Discipling happened for one hour per week during class. When we were done with the class, we were done with the discipling until next week. I simply wasn't paying attention to Jesus beyond that.

However, the gospels show us that *life* is Jesus' discipling classroom. With this simple mindset shift, discipling goes from an hour per week to hour after hour throughout the week. The difference is huge. It is similar to the difference we would experience if we practiced a foreign language an hour per week versus being immersed in it on a daily basis. In the same way, Jesus invites us into his immersion program. He invites us to be discipled by him day after day as we join him on his mission along life's way.

So let's pay attention.

On the other hand, in the gospels we also see Jesus using another kind of classroom. He regularly takes his disciples out of the melee of daily mission and discipling and leads them to quieter places. He gives them time and space for reflection and conversation. Jesus uses both kinds of classrooms. He uses the "classroom of everyday life" to give his followers real-life experience and he uses the "classroom of time together" for reflection and conversation so that they can sort out what they have experienced and learned.

We see Jesus creating this "classroom of time together" when he gets into a boat with his disciples and heads to the other side of the lake to get away from the crowds (Mark 4:36, 6:32). We see him creating this "classroom" when Jesus goes into houses where they can privately reflect on his teaching and ask their own questions (Mark 7:17). We see it when Jesus takes advantage of the time it takes to travel by foot in order to talk with his disciples about what is happening and what it means (Mark 8:27). We see it in how Jesus regularly uses the Garden of Gethsemane as a place where he and his disciples can take a breather, talk, reflect and pray (John 18:2; Luke 22:39; Mark 14:32).

In the book *Joining Jesus on His Mission*, we refer to this "classroom of time together" as "Missional Community" (see chapter nineteen of that book). Missional Community provides a regular time for Jesus-followers like us to step out of the busyness of everyday life and come together in a place where we can take a breather, have some time for reflection and conversation and sort out what we are learning from Jesus on our mission adventure with him.

In Missional Community, we help each other in the same way the writer to the Hebrews encouraged the Jesus-followers of his day to help each other: "And let us consider how we may spur one another on toward love and good deeds. Let us not give up meeting together, as some are in the habit of doing, but let us encourage one another—and all the more as you see the Day approaching" (Hebrew 10:24-25).

To prompt the kind of reflection and conversation we see in the gospels and Hebrews 10 encourages, Dwelling 1:14 advocates using the 5 Questions. (The 5 Questions are based on the 5 Mission Practices and are listed in this book at the end of the introduction.) The 5 Questions simply prompt us to sort out and tell our stories of what we are learning as we live our life on mission with Jesus. Where else do we have the opportunity to gather with friends and help one another sort out and clarify the stories that we have? Gathering regularly to tell our stories and hear the stories of our friends is what keeps us encouraged, informed, focused and accountable for living life with Jesus as a daily lifestyle. Dwelling 1:14's experience with thousands of Jesus-followers is that if they regularly engage with one another in Missional Community, they see growth and fruit on a regular basis. On the other hand, if Jesus-followers start to "give up meeting together, as some are in the habit of doing," the priority of joining Jesus in daily life fades and they generally go back to normal very quickly.

Simply put, we need a little help from our friends.

There are a variety of ways we can engage in Missional Community:

1. **The Family:**

   The family is the God-created classroom for children. The Bible says (and studies confirm) that the most powerful discipling influence in a young child's life—by far—is not a pastor or a Sunday School teacher, it is the parents. The parents' lifestyle is the object lesson their kids use to make sense of all they see and hear. The lifestyle of the parents—what they value and how they live day after day—shapes the kids more deeply and permanently than any other influence, for better or worse. Church programming can supplement what parents are doing during the week to disciple their children but it cannot substitute for it. The family is the God-created classroom that trains the child's thinking, attitudes and behaviors regarding life with Jesus for the long term.

A simple but powerful way to be more intentional about discipling as a family is to take time to be a Missional Community as a family. As you go along life's way, ask one another the 5 Questions. "What did you see Jesus up to today? How did you respond? What do you think you could do tomorrow?" In other words, give one another a prompt to reflect, recognize and then tell the story of how life with Jesus is going. This can happen during a family meal, a walk, a drive or before going to bed (see Deuteronomy 6). Hearing and telling the stories of life with Jesus is an exercise kids need so that they can reframe all they have seen and heard during the day with Jesus in the middle.

2. **Existing Congregational Groups:**

    Are you already part of the choir, a committee, a Bible study, a small group or a ministry team? Ask the leader for permission to do what we call "Take-10." Before the group engages the regular agenda, take 10 minutes, break into small groups of two or three people and ask a prompting question (for instance, one of the 5 Questions). Each person gets three to five minutes to reflect and tell his/her story. After the 10 minutes is up, move on to the rest of the meeting. But in the meantime you have helped disciple your group to join Jesus on his mission. Ten minutes isn't much, but we have seen important progress made with people when we regularly give them even this brief opportunity for reflection and conversation.

3. **Other Missionaries in the "Neighborhood":**

Have you met other likeminded Jesus-followers where you live, work or go to school? Invite them to regularly gather with you in order to support one another in Missional Community. For instance, if you know other Jesus-followers at work, you can invite them to meet in a coffee shop on Monday mornings before work in order to tell the stories of what Jesus was up to last week in the workplace and how you might respond this week. You can pray together for the boss or for people who are particularly difficult. "Thy kingdom come, thy will be done right here in the company as it is in heaven." You can hold one another up as you head into another week, seeking opportunities to be a reason something good happens in the lives of fellow workers. You can also do this where you live or where you go to school. Of course, if you have fellow church members who live, work or go to school with you, they can be a part of the mission team too!

By the way, here's an important tip about how to form community and friendship in a group: Experience shows that if we first focus on building community/friendship in our group—thinking we can introduce mission engagement sometime later—it slows down actual engagement in personal mission by *years*. Groups tend to enjoy the friendship they build, while routinely putting off "personal mission engagement" until sometime down the road. And "sometime" usually turns into years. On the other hand, if a group focuses on personal mission engagement from the beginning, with a priority on telling and hearing their stories, friendship follows—and ironically it is achieved sooner and at a deeper level than the groups who solely focus on friendship. Why? There is something about telling the stories of our real-life struggles and adventures with Jesus that accelerates the deepening of friendship.

And that is the primary difference between a Missional Community and any other small group at church: the stories we tell. Both kinds of groups value God's Word, prayer and friendship. But in Missional Community we get to do more than share our correct answers or abstract responses to questions asked in a booklet. We get to share our stories of real-life with Jesus and encourage one another as we head out for another week of adventuring with him.

Several months ago, my wife, Susan, helped start a "Bible study" with some young ladies from the neighborhood. What made this interesting was that, except for Susan, none of the ladies had ever been in a Bible study before. However, over the years, our neighbors have all been cultivating friendship with one another. They enjoy one another and trust one another. So while the ladies were nervous about it, they were also ready to take this next step together.

Since none of them had been in a Bible study before, Susan invited them to consider doing the study in such a way that they would learn about the Bible *and* learn how to live life with Jesus every day. In other words, she invited them to become a Missional Community and be discipled in the ways of Jesus. They now gather every week. When they arrive they take time to reconnect and catch up. They are not in a hurry. Eventually Susan starts inviting stories. "So what's Jesus been up to this week? In your family? At work? What parts of his Word have helped you or challenged you along the way?" And the stories come— and the questions, and the encouragement, and the insight, and the accountability. And you should see how they are growing!

When the group first started meeting, the women had never

considered that Jesus would want to be involved in their lives beyond a church service. They didn't read the Bible regularly. Some didn't even own one. They didn't pray regularly with their children or at all with their husbands. They didn't know how to seek the kingdom of God or join Jesus on his mission. Now they do. They are being discipled. They just needed someone to show them how and a regular space in which to gather and sort things through. At the end of the evening, when the women head for their homes, they know their discipling with Jesus has not ended but that it has just begun for another week. And they are showing their children, their husbands and even other friends how to do the same.

A couple weeks ago, one of the women came to the Missional Community with a new insight she wanted to share. Shelley had been reading her Bible and came across Hebrews 10:24-25: "And let us consider how we may spur one another on toward love and good deeds. Let us not give up meeting together, as some are in the habit of doing, but let us encourage one another—and all the more as you see the Day approaching." As she finished reading the verses, she looked at her friends with wonder on her face and said, "This is us!"

Yes, it is, Shelley. Yes, it is.

That's what Missional Community has fostered. With a little help from their friends in the "classroom" of Missional Community, the women are better able to recognize and pay attention to what Jesus is showing them in the "classroom" of everyday life. And the fruits are showing up. They have Jesus-stories now. They are enjoying deeper friendships, more robust faith and closer family ties as they seek to join Jesus every day.

Jesus disciples the women every day and Susan gets to help once a week.

And soon you and I will be able to do the same in our little part of his kingdom.

HERE'S THE POINT

In the gospels Jesus does most of his discipling in the midst of his daily mission adventure. He then takes his disciples to quieter places where they can have time for reflection and conversation. The "classroom" of daily life helps his followers gain experiences and understanding. The "classroom" of time together helps them reflect and sort out what they have experienced and learned with him. And we can do the same.

CHAPTER 13
WHAT IS JESUS'
DISCIPLING CURRICULUM?

"Of course he isn't safe. But he's good."

—*Mr. Beaver describing King Aslan the Lion*

Life as a follower of Jesus is not safe and it is not comfortable. But it is good.

Jesus lays that out for us when he says, "If anyone would come after me, he must deny himself and take up his cross and follow me. For whoever wants to save his life will lose it, but whoever loses his life for me will find it. What good will it be for a man if he gains the whole world, yet forfeits his soul?" (Matthew 16:24-25).

Joining Jesus on his mission costs us our lives. But it is a good transaction because, in the process of losing our lives, we finally gain lives that are truly fulfilled and fruitful. We, of course, don't trust this intuitively. At least, not at first. We need to be trained (discipled) by Jesus to gain such confidence. Being trained *by* Jesus gives us the critical experience we need *with* Jesus to have more confidence *in* Jesus.

Makes sense.

However, in order to achieve that level of training and confidence, Jesus uses a very specific curriculum. What is it?

To put it simply, Jesus uses *himself* as the curriculum.

Earlier we saw that Jesus trains his followers through a process of Proclamation, Imitation/Participation and Replication. He tells them what they need to know and then invites them to follow him so they can watch him and imitate his practices for the good of others. These same followers then show others how to do the same. And Jesus is the curriculum.

We also saw earlier that the Bible gives us three main places where we can watch Jesus and then imitate him:

1. in the gospels;

2. in daily life;

3. and in the lives of other experienced Jesus-followers.

That means all three of these should be included in our discipling curriculum. But what does that look like?

Unfortunately, over the last several centuries, the church has been steadily reducing its discipling curriculum to little more than written materials. Written materials are preferred because they are efficient. You can hand them out, have them read and test retention very efficiently. The problem, of course, is that written materials alone can't train us. They are part of the training curriculum—we need to know what is written—but we are not trained by written materials. Written materials alone are no more effective at training Jesus-followers than is sheet music at training musicians or is an anatomy textbook at training surgeons. Music students certainly need sheet music and medical students need anatomy textbooks. But the best training curriculum is a *person* who shows in real life what the written materials tell us on the page.

So if we want to disciple our family and friends using Jesus' *full* curriculum, we will certainly guide them to the written words of the gospels and help them look for Jesus at work in everyday life; but they also need a close relationship with someone who is an experienced Jesus-follower so they can *see* what living life with Jesus looks like. And that "someone" is *you*. Remember, the best training curriculum is a *person* who shows in real life what is written on the page. However, experience shows that cultivating such a relationship is easy to shortchange and put off. It is the part of Jesus' discipling curriculum that takes the most effort (even within our own families). But if we want Jesus' discipling results, doesn't it make sense to follow his full discipling curriculum?

Last Father's Day I was reminded of this by something my high school biology teacher posted to Facebook. He posted it in honor of his late father. My teacher's name is Mark Baacke (Little Baacke to generations of his students) and he expresses in his post the reason why investing ourselves in the ones we are discipling is so critical.

"Twenty years ago today my dad went home to heaven. He taught me how to play golf, ping pong, baseball and how to make a game out of any situation I faced. He taught me always to do my best even at things I didn't like too much (history, English, washing the car, etc.). When something seemed impossible and I felt like quitting, he would say, 'That's no hill for a climber.' Or when a situation totally sucked or was unfair, he'd tell me, 'Sometimes it goes like that for days, and then it gets worse.' I don't recall him ever telling me to be a teacher, but he was such a good teacher himself that I grew up wanting to do what he did. He was serious about the important things in life, but he would be the first one to laugh when life threw him a curveball. He had the ability to see right through fake people. I think the little kid in the story about the emperor's new clothes probably grew up to be my dad. He loved his country and made it better by being a good man himself.

"Most importantly, he loved his Lord and Savior, and the more I think about my dad, the more I realize how many times and in how many ways he was letting me see that love in the way he treated people and the way he went through life. Over these past 20 years there are lots of memories and images of my dad that have stayed with me, but one keeps coming up more than most. I'm an eight-year-old kid, and dad is taking me fishing. There are tall weeds between where we parked the car and the pond where we're going to fish. Dad goes ahead of me and I try to follow, but soon he's lost from sight, and I'm surrounded by weeds that are twice as tall as I am. We've done this before, and he's taught me not to panic but just to follow the trail of bent and broken weeds. So that's what I do until I reach the pond and find him smiling back at me because he knows where I'll pop out of the weeds. And so it's been 20 years now that I've been walking through the weeds of life without him, but I've got his trail to follow because he intentionally did things to help me see it, and I firmly believe he was following a trail that Jesus left for him. So one day I'll pop out of the weeds and Jesus will be waiting for me with Dad right there with him."

Yep. That's what we're talking about. If we're going to follow Jesus' discipling curriculum, we will need to move beyond programs and start investing *ourselves* in the ones we are discipling. As the experienced Jesus-followers, we are the ones who have been this way before with Jesus. We are the ones who can show them what life with Jesus looks like. We are their object lessons. It's a part of Jesus' discipling curriculum we simply cannot leave out.

What are some of the factors in building this kind of relationship?

1. Carve out time and space for it.

This kind of relationship requires us to invest regular time with the people we are discipling. Without it, there is probably very little discipling actually happening. Jesus loved the crowds and gave much of himself to the crowds. But he regularly carved out time for the 12 and even more time for the three (Peter, James and John). This is our Missional Community time.

2. **As Dallas Willard advises, "Ruthlessly eliminate hurry from your life."**

It is almost impossible to disciple someone when we're in a hurry. We can't be in a hurry if we are really going to hear what a person is saying. We can't be in a hurry if we're going to walk with them as they work through the next insight or challenge Jesus is offering. Ironically, going slow is the fastest way to disciple a person. Fast and efficient is usually ineffective.

3. **Be happy to see the one you are discipling.**

As simple as that sounds, it has a huge effect. Research shows that when the person we are discipling experiences our joy and love, he/she is more deeply impacted by our character and training. On the other hand, the more emotionally sterile the "relationship" is the less impact we have.

4. **Tell stories.**

Brain researchers are beginning to understand what regular folks have always known: there is something powerful about a simple story. According to scientists, hearing a story causes the empathetic portion of our brains to light up. The brains of the storyteller and the one hearing the story literally synchronize with each other. When I say, "Let me tell you the story of what happened last week," it is like saying, "I know you couldn't be there, so let me take you back with me." In other words, it will be like we are there together. Telling and hearing the stories are powerful tools for discipling our kids, friends and fellow church members.

5. **Finally, offer regular, unhurried access to your life as the experienced Jesus-follower.**

The person being discipled needs access to us so they can tell us their stories, hear our stories, ask their questions, sort through their thoughts and experiences, learn from their mistakes and come to new insights and decisions. With this renewed clarity, they can then go out and imitate our ways as an experienced Jesus-follower in their own life.

Jo Saxton, a discipleship veteran, reminds us, "Imitation requires access to your life." And the most helpful access we can offer is full access. This means access to both our wins and misses, strengths and weaknesses, struggles and breakthroughs, sin and repentance. Such access and honesty fosters an "into-me-see" level of trust and discipleship. A friend of mine from South Africa named Bradly introduced me to this phrase many years ago. "Intimacy" means "into-me-see." It is allowing another to see into my life—as it is—for the sake of building both trust and understanding for how life with Jesus really works.

Of course, being transparent as the "more experienced Jesus-follower" is not exactly comfortable. We fear looking weak or revealing our shortcomings. However, the truth is, the ones we are discipling usually have more clarity about our shortcomings than we do! (Especially if they are our children.) Besides, how does real growth happen? By being perfect? By never falling short? By always choosing correctly? Of course not. Our best growth generally happens after we have fallen down. The goal of discipling is to train people to remember their true identity and join Jesus every day. So falling down no longer needs to be failure, it can become training. Falling down is only failure if we give up and quit. Falling down and getting up wiser is training. As uncomfortable as it may be, our falling-down stories can be a rich source of wisdom and training for others.

By now, if you are like 99% of Christians in the U.S., there is probably another challenge that is causing your chest to tighten right about now: the challenge of time. We wonder, "Who has time for this?!" Jesus gets that.

In Mark 6:30-34, the disciples have just returned from a brief mission exercise, and they have new stories to sort through with Jesus. But the demands of the growing crowds are getting so crazy they don't even have time to eat, much less discuss their stories. The daily crush is making it almost impossible to find time for reflection and conversation. (Sound familiar?) So what does Jesus do? He doesn't cave to the busyness. He makes a decision. They get in the boat and go to a quiet place where they could get some rest and sort through their stories. And how does Jesus come to this decision? Simple. He has previously set priorities (Matthew 4:19). When life gets crazy, honoring previously set priorities is what keeps us on course. In Mark 6, there was much to do and much Jesus *could* do. That's why he had set a priority for what he *had* to do—disciple his followers. So when the busyness threatened to overwhelm the discipling, Jesus made the decision: "It's time to go." And they left the crowds and got in the boat.

Spending unhurried time discipling our kids, friends or fellow church members doesn't require all of our time or even a majority of our time. However, it does require a priority of our time. If we want to see our family and friends discipled, we will need to set it as a priority like Jesus did. And if we don't? We need to be honest and say that we are willing to leave our family and friends under-discipled. It's that simple. Jesus' discipling curriculum requires that we invest ourselves in the people we are discipling.

Finally, many of us will also struggle with the idea of someone "imitating" our life. We think, "Honestly, what do I have to imitate anyway?" And that's correct. On our own, we have so many shortcomings and deficits of character that the thought of others watching us and imitating us seems like a really bad idea. In fact we are so messed up there is literally only one thing we have to offer worth imitating at all—Jesus. Jesus is all we have to offer. A little of his love, good news, humility and self-sacrificing service is all we have worth imitating. But don't miss this: it is gold. It is not only worth imitating, it is the hope of the world. Think if all the Christians on the face of the earth got over the fact that they are not perfect and only have Jesus to offer... and then they simply offered Jesus. It would be a great day for the world.

Think if all the 2.2 billion Christians on the face of the earth began to offer a little of his love, good news, humility and self-sacrificing service to the people around them... and then did it daily... habitually... as a lifestyle... because this is who we are and this is what we do. The mission of redeeming and restoring the world would take a quantum leap forward.

And it's not a pipedream. We can start and then we can turn and disciple others to do the same—our children, friends, neighbors and fellow church members. We have the curriculum. Now all we need to do is make it the priority.

HERE'S THE POINT

Jesus' discipling curriculum is Jesus. The Bible gives us three main places where we can watch Jesus and then imitate him:

1. in the gospels;

2. in everyday life with him;

3. and in relationships with other experienced Jesus-followers.

Wouldn't we be wise to follow the same curriculum as we disciple our family and friends?

And that brings us to the end of Part 1, "Regaining Clarity and Simplicity for How Jesus Disciples His Followers in the Gospels."

In chapter one, we noted that the reason why many of us are afraid of discipling others is because we misunderstand what discipling is. We have an unclear, academic presumption about what discipling must be. So in Part 1, we followed Jesus around in the gospels in order to clarify and simplify in our minds how he disciples his followers. In Part 2, we will use that clarity and simplicity in order to put together our own plan for discipling our children, friends, neighbors and fellow church members with intentionality and consistency. Let's get started!

PART 2

Crafting Your Discipling Plan

CHAPTER 14
HOW DO I START?

*"There is a time when every good idea
disintegrates into hard work."*

—*The voice of experience*

So, what do we actually *do* with all this "discipling clarity" we are gaining?

I remember when Susan and I faced that question for the first time. We had been gaining clarity about how Jesus disciples his followers in the gospels. The blinding flashes of the obvious were coming, and we wanted to incorporate those insights into how we discipled people. Unfortunately, all of our practical experience was in leading various classes and programs at church. When it came to discipling the way Jesus did in the gospels, we were still rookies. So we invited a group of our neighbors, who were also fellow church members, to start gathering with us once a week so that we could figure it out together. We eventually started calling those gatherings "Missional Communities."

That was nearly 10 years ago.

Since that first Missional Community, various friends have come together with Susan and me over the years. We continued discovering more and more of what Jesus had already been showing us in the gospels about mission and discipling. (These "blinding flashes of the obvious" make up the content of Part 1.) But that was only the first part of what we learned. Our Missional Communities also wrestled with figuring out the *practicalities* of imitating Jesus' discipling plan with real people, in real life, in the 21st century. We experimented, evaluated and slowly gained experience. We made plenty of mistakes too. But as we made mistakes, we also learned; and several practical lessons emerged.

What did we learn?

Over the next four chapters, we will share the following practical lessons:

1. How to get started discipling a person or a group of people.

2. 5 Discipling Practices that optimize the time you have in Missional Community.

3. A simple template you can use to craft a plan for discipling your children, friends, neighbors or fellow church members.

4. A few personal practices that you would be wise to engage as the one doing the discipling. (These personal practices are for your sake as well as for the sake of the person you are discipling.)

So how do you get started discipling a person or a group of people? It's an easy question to underestimate. However, starting well can help you avoid several unnecessary setbacks and frustrations. Here are some best practices:

1. **Start with the End in Mind**

   If you start discipling people without a clear plan for where you want to end up, it's very easy to veer off course and start wandering in the wilderness together. Instead start with the end clearly in mind like Jesus did. When Jesus says, "Come, follow me, and I will make you fishers of men," he is indicating where he wants his followers to end up: namely, participating in the mission of God as a daily lifestyle. And that's where we want to end up too. The template in chapter sixteen will help you craft your discipling plan so that the end stays clearly in mind.

2. **Prioritize Your Schedule around Discipling**

Before you reach out to disciple people, reach out for a calendar. As noted, discipling doesn't require a majority of your time but it does require a priority of your time. Experience shows that hurrying through your time together or regularly postponing it because you are overbooked simply doesn't work. A lack of priority results in a lack of effectiveness. So before you start inviting people to be discipled, look at your own schedule and prioritize at least two hours per week for it (or if you are discipling your child, prioritize a little time every day).

3. **Identify the Person You will be Discipling**

This may sound obvious, but the only people you can disciple are the people who want you to disciple them. If they are unmotivated to be discipled, little progress can be made. So who is willing and ready? If you are a parent, your first responsibility, of course, is to disciple your child. Beyond that, who wants to be with you, learn from you and imitate the Jesus they see in you? Start with them. (See #5 below for how to invite a person into a discipling relationship or group.)

4. **Think Long-Term Relationship not Short-Term Program**

As I write this, news is breaking of the death of golfing great Arnold Palmer. Though many accolades are pouring in, something I heard from Jack Nicklaus really stood out. He said of Arnold Palmer, "He shepherded me." Arnold Palmer was already a great professional golfer when Jack Nicklaus burst on the scene in 1961. Arnold was talented and seasoned. Jack was talented but a rookie. Arnold could have ignored him or treated him like a rival. But instead he took Jack under his wing and "shepherded" him in the game of golf and in the game of life. Over the decades, they became dear friends.

That's what discipling offers. The influence Arnold Palmer had on Jack Nicklaus was not because of a short-term program he conducted on how to play golf (or life) but because of his willingness to invest in a long-term relationship. So as you prepare to invite someone to be discipled, think of it as an invitation into a discipling friendship rather than simply a discipling program or class. Of course no one can guarantee how a friendship will go before you even start. However, experience shows that when you have such an attitude you are starting well.

5. **Give the Gift of Clear Expectations**

Many discipling plans veer off course right away because the invitation we offer lacks clarity regarding expectations. Two common mistakes are made: 1) we invite people to be discipled before we have a clear discipling plan (and soon find ourselves wandering in the wilderness together); or 2) we want them to say "yes" so badly that we shy away from clearly stating our true expectations. Either mistake will soon cause frustration in the discipling relationship because the expectations of the two people are unclear and unaligned. With this kind of start, experience shows that the discipling relationship will be in danger of falling apart right away. Instead give the gift of clear expectations. There is no secret about what the process of discipling requires for it to actually work. So be clear about that in your invitation. An example is the following:

I would like to invite you into a discipling relationship with me [or into a discipling group with me] for the next 10 weeks [or whatever number of weeks it will be]. Our goal will be to learn how to seek God's kingdom and join Jesus' mission as part of our everyday lives. Are you interested?

(Sure, what does it involve?)

I'd like for you to do three things:

1. *Every day, I would like for you to follow Jesus around in one of the gospels and take note of what he gives you to believe and do. Don't worry about what you don't understand. Just take note of what you do understand. I will do the same thing.*

2. *I would like for you to then look for opportunities throughout the day to put Jesus' beliefs and practices into play for the good of others. I will do the same thing.*

3. *Once a week, you and I will meet together [or meet together with our group, or meet via FaceTime, etc.] to talk through what we have experienced as we sought to follow Jesus in everyday life.*

We will do that as best we can for the next [several] weeks and see what Jesus teaches us. We can then decide if we want to continue or call it good.

Such an invitation is winsome, but still gives people the opportunity to make an honest choice about whether or not they are ready to take up the process of becoming a trained follower of Jesus.

6. **Ask about Baptism**

Finally, as you get started, be sure to ask the person you will be discipling whether they are baptized in the name of Jesus. If they are not, then talk with them about Matthew 28:19 and how, according to Jesus, baptism is the first step in becoming his disciple.

So these are some of the best insights Susan and I have for starting well: clarity, priority, willingness, relationship, invitation and baptism. That's how we get started. Now let's turn our attention to making the most of our discipling time.

HERE'S THE POINT

How do we get started discipling a person or a group of people? It's an easy question to underestimate. However, starting well can help us avoid several unnecessary setbacks and frustrations. This chapter offers some of the best insights we have learned over the years.

CHAPTER 15
5 DISCIPLING PRACTICES— MAKING THE MOST OF OUR DISCIPLING TIME

"So don't whisper softly the things you want loudly to be."

—*Tyler Stenson, songwriter*

I never saw it coming.

As I sat in the passenger seat of this 75-year-old grandma's aging Buick, I was about to have the ride of my life.

Over the weekend I had been speaking at a women's mission conference in Eugene, Oregon. The conference had ended at 11:00 A.M. on Sunday and I was scheduled to lead a training workshop at a church in Portland later that afternoon. So in order to save me money on a rental car, this gracious senior had volunteered to drive me back to Portland. I anticipated an uneventful two-hour ride at a reasonable pace (read: within the posted speed limits).

I was wrong. On both counts.

After I put on my seatbelt, she carefully shifted the car into drive and eased her big Buick out of the parking lot. Once we were on I-5 heading north to Portland, she glanced at me and said, "If we hurry,

I can take you on some back roads and show you our beautiful wine country. Would you like that?" I asked, "Can we do that and still make it back to Portland in time?" She answered with a gleam in her eye and a slight smile on her face, "We sure can." And with that, this 75-year-old church lady literally put the pedal to the metal!

Leaving others in the dust, we sped along the interstate for several miles. When she saw the exit she was looking for, we got off the interstate and headed into the hills. Quickly. And she was right. It *was* beautiful. It was June and the hills between Eugene and Portland were filled with one picturesque vineyard after another. And she was eager to show me it all. But to do so she had to race along the back roads at speeds that would make any Formula One driver proud.

The roads twisted left and right, up and down. Each corner took my breath away, both because of the speed at which we took them but also because of the next view that was revealed. If I lived, I would have some beautiful memories! And then, unexpectedly, she decelerated. We had entered a wide valley and just up the road was a little place she knew of. As she eased into the parking lot, she said, "I always take a pit stop here." The place was an unexpected wonderland. It was a cornucopia of garden produce, crafts, flowering plants and baked goods. My adventurous friend also knew it was hosting an annual event called The BBQ, Berries and Brew Festival.

I partook of two of the three offerings. (She insisted.)

After we got our plate of food and glass of brew, we were directed outside where the land and the view opened up. People were sitting at picnic tables, relaxing and visiting, while an artist played his guitar and sang. It was a surreal experience. Moments before I had been flying white-knuckled through this picturesque landscape. Now I was sitting in it, enjoying some music, some surprisingly good BBQ and a little something from a local craft brewery.

I turned to Speed Racer and asked, "Do we have time for this?" She looked at me disapprovingly and replied, "Of course we have time. Now, take a deep breath and enjoy your surroundings."

So I did. And when I did, I discovered something. (Like I said, I never saw it coming.) Jesus had evidently brought me here for a reason. It wasn't just for the beauty, or the BBQ or the brew. It was for the song. Turns out the artist singing was Tyler Stenson, an award-winning singer/songwriter from Portland. (Clearly the event planners were serious about the entertainment they brought in.) When I heard the words he was singing, one of the lines really settled on me. It went like this, "When it's the end of the line—and your train has rolled through the time—all your graces and legacies stand. So don't whisper softly the things you want loudly to be."

The song wasn't a Christian song or even particularly spiritual. And yet it was. "Don't whisper softly the things you want loudly to be." I scrambled to find something to write with so I wouldn't lose the words. There was something there. Jesus was messing with me through the lyrics.

As we got back in the Buick and continued to Portland, I hardly noticed our breakneck speed any more because: 1) I had come to trust my friend's skill as a Formula One driver; and 2) I was busy rolling those lyrics around in my head. Through it Jesus seemed to be wrestling with me about legacy, about seeing the end from the beginning, about limited time, about clarity and priority, about intentionality and consistency. And then I realized. There was a parallel here for me about how I was leaving my legacy with my family and friends and how I was discipling them. If I wanted to leave a legacy of family and friends who were filled with Jesus' love, joy, peace and patience, if I wanted to leave a legacy of them seeking his kingdom and joining him on his mission, then I couldn't whisper softly the things I wanted loudly to be. Instead I needed to disciple them on purpose.

If you too would like to leave such a legacy, don't whisper softly the things you want loudly to be. Make the most of your time with your family and friends and disciple them on purpose. Here's how.

Over the years Susan and I have found that the best opportunity we have for discipling our family and friends on purpose is during our Missional Community time. But that time is also limited. So we have learned the importance of *optimizing* our time together for the purpose of discipling. We do that by using 5 Discipling Practices that help us purposefully frame and direct the conversation toward our discipling outcomes. You can think of them as best practices for your Missional Community toolbox.

The 5 Discipling Practices are the following:

1. **True Identity and Mission in Christ**

   Every week we start our time together by reminding each other, "Remember: This is who we are in Christ. This is what we have in Christ. This is what we do in Christ." This practice is our #1 priority.

   Why is it #1? Because it's really easy to get overwhelmed by everyday life and forget who we are, what we have and what our purpose is. So it's essential that during every gathering of our Missional Community we watch for opportunities to remind each other, "Through baptism into Christ, our true identity and mission have been restored. Who are we? We are beloved children of the Heavenly King! What do we have? We have the things of his kingdom and in abundance! What do we do? We look for people who need a little bit of what we already have in abundance and offer it to them." This is most certainly true.

Being reminded of this is also important because the devil is constantly trying to tempt us away from it. Just as the devil tried to tempt Jesus away from remembering his true identity and mission (see Luke 4:1-12), he also tries to tempt us away. But just like Jesus, we can counter the devil's lies with the Father's truth. Ever since Jesus died on the cross and rose again, the devil no longer has any real power over us. All he has are lies, which have no power whatsoever when we already know the truth. The truth sets us free. Unfortunately, the devil is persistent. In Luke 4:13, even though Jesus had successfully rebuffed the temptations of the devil, there is still this ominous warning: "When the devil had finished all this tempting, he left Jesus until an opportune time." The devil is our enemy too, and he plays dirty. He watches for opportune times to slide back in and start his lying all over again. But "we are not unaware of his schemes" (2 Corinthians 2:11). So we remind each other often of our "True Identity and Mission in Christ." This is who we are. This is what we have. This is what we do.

2. In Here Is for Out There

"In here is for out there" is also a practice of reminding. We look for opportunities during our Missional Community to remind each other that what we do and experience "in here" with our group has its focus and purpose "out there" in our daily lives. We practice reminding each other of this for three reasons:

It's easy to focus on ourselves "in here" and forget about the mission of God "out there." In this 21st century, it is normal for North American Christians to gather together and be entirely focused on each other. We love to form and maintain "holy huddles." We love to care for each other. We long to feel comfortable with people like ourselves. And that is fine. But that is not the point of the Missional Community. The reason we gather in here is to help each other focus on the mission of God out there where people still need the grace and truth of Jesus. So every time we gather, we remind each other, "In here is for out there."

What we experience "in here" can be immediately replicated "out there" for discipling others. Remember, Jesus' discipling process has three parts: Proclamation, Imitation/Participation and Replication. "In here is for out there" also reminds us to immediately take the discipling experiences we are having inside the group and begin replicating them with our family or friends outside the group. In other words, what we do in here with our Missional Community can be immediately replicated out there for the sake of discipling more people. If we stop fostering Replication, we have essentially stopped discipling the way Jesus does. So, every week toward the end of your Missional Community time, take a moment to ask, "What small part of our experience today can you replicate with your family or friends during the coming week?"

If we don't multiply our group for the sake of discipling more people, who will? Finally, "in here is for out there" can be used to prepare our group to multiply from one Missional Community to two (or more). Why do we need to keep multiplying Missional Communities? Because to pursue the Great Commission of Jesus, we need to continue increasing capacity for more and more people to be discipled through relationships with other everyday missionaries. If we don't, who will? And we know that the most effective discipling happens not in big groups but in the context of smaller groups like the Missional Community offers—thus the need for multiplying small groups in order to increase this kind of capacity. Having said that, even the most mission-minded people can be reluctant to multiply their Missional Community. So experience has taught us the necessity of championing the goal of multiplication with the group every week. We remind each other that it is a win for our group and the Great Commission when we grow from one group to two (or more).

Another important way to prepare for multiplication is by having the group watch for who among them seems to be emerging as a new Missional Community leader. Likewise, consider which individuals may be ready to go with a new leader—all for the sake of Jesus' Great Commission. Certainly multiplication of the Missional Community will not happen often, but we remind each other often that this is our goal.

3. **Ask Good Questions**

What good are "Good Questions?"

"Good Questions" prompt real stories and real biblical insights. The most important part of the Missional Community experience is our reflection and conversation about how life on mission with Jesus is going. But for that to happen, we need some "Good Questions" to prompt us. "Good Questions" help us recall what happened last week as we lived our lives on mission with Jesus. When we tell our stories, biblical concepts become concrete for us, biblical truths take on flesh and blood and we see how biblical theology applies in real life. To prompt these stories and insights, we advocate using the 5 Questions from the book *Joining Jesus on His Mission*:

- **How did you see God at work in your life this week?** What has he been up to around you? Who has he been bringing across your path? Who is he inviting you to pay attention to?

- **What has God been teaching you in his Word?** As you followed Jesus around in the gospels this week, what did he invite you to believe or do? What happened for the good of others when you put it into practice?

- **What kind of conversations are you having with your pre-Christian friends?** A conversation with anyone God brings across your path is important. But a conversation with someone living without the grace and truth of Jesus is especially important. What did you learn about the person's story? What aspect of the good news of Jesus would be a cool cup of water to him or her? What might be the next step in your interactions?

- **What good can you do?**
  As you reflect on last week's observations and conversations with the people around you, how can you serve, bless or encourage someone next week? What's their name? What's your plan? How can we help?

- **What do you want us to ask you about next week and how can we help you in prayer?**

With these 5 Questions prompting your Missional Community, the stories start to flow and so do the insights. Of course these are not the only "Good Questions" you can ask. However, they have proven to be effective at keeping reflections and conversations rooted in the reality of what Jesus is actually up to in the lives of real people who really need his grace and truth.

A reminder to celebrate small steps: As people tell their stories, be sure to value and celebrate their small acts and baby steps. Why? The Bible tells us to. Zechariah 4:10, "Who despises the day of small things?" Matthew 13:31, "The kingdom of God is like a mustard seed." Throughout the Bible, God cautions us not to underestimate the importance and power of small, humble things. He cautions us because, in fact, that's how he goes about most of his work. In the kingdom of God, small is big. Least is greatest. Last is first. A seed eventually becomes a tree. A pinch of yeast eventually fills the loaf. A cool cup of water eventually becomes a river of living water. Zechariah 4:6 says, "'Not by might nor by power, but by my Spirit,' says the LORD Almighty." 1 Corinthians 1:27 says, "But God chose the foolish things of the world to shame the wise; God chose the weak things of the world to shame the strong." It's how God rolls. So let's join him in championing the small acts and baby steps our family and friends take and then encourage the telling of those stories in our Missional Community.

A warning to beware of coasting into boredom: Even though we are asking "Good Questions" and inviting stories week after week, sometimes the people we are discipling can still slip from actively joining Jesus to simply coasting. They get busy; they get distracted; they get a little lax. Whatever the cause, it happens. And when it happens: the person's or group's real-life stories start to dry up. They start settling for abstract discussions... which after a week or two becomes a little stale and boring... which then leads to a suggestion that perhaps the group should start "studying" something new. Don't be fooled. There is a simple cause for this boredom. Call it what it is. They have stopped seeking the kingdom and joining Jesus on his mission. The remedy is simple too. Repent, believe the good news and start following Jesus again in the new week (see Mark 1:15-17). When coasting starts to happen, take a moment to look each other in the eye and gently say, "Jesus didn't get stale and boring over the last couple of weeks—we did. Jesus didn't stop working in our neighborhoods. We stopped seeking and responding. We stopped noticing and serving people. We've started coasting. This week let's recommit to seeking the kingdom of God first of all. Let's recommit to noticing the people around us and joining Jesus on his mission." And then have the group pray for it to happen: "Jesus, give us eyes that are seeking, ears that are listening and hearts that are ready to respond to the people you have prepared around us."

The stories will start to flow again the next week. Guaranteed.

"Good Questions" prompt effective training: Beyond prompting our mission stories, "Good Questions" also prompt actual experience and training. When we begin discipling people in Missional Community, they are usually inexperienced in speaking about their life with Jesus in a natural, casual way. They may have lots of experience talking about faith abstractly in a Bible class. But talking about their personal faith with a friend or neighbor in everyday life?? (Yikes!) Likewise, they are probably inexperienced in praying out loud with other people. They may have lots of experience with pastors praying for them at church. But praying with a neighbor in a driveway?? (Double yikes!) However, "Good Questions" during our Missional Community prompt effective training in these areas. How?

Noted outreach expert Leroy Biesenthal once wrote, "Indeed, I have repeatedly suggested that one of the reasons we in the [church] find it so difficult to talk to others about Jesus is that we rarely talk to each other about him in a natural, casual, spontaneous way." In other words, we lack experience talking even with each other about Jesus! Our experience consists of coming to church and listening to experts talk about Jesus for us. However, in our Missional Community, when we ask

"Good Questions," it prompts us to reflect and then talk *with each other* about what happened last week with Jesus (aka, our witness). The more we reflect and tell our stories to each other week after week, the more experience we gain and the more natural it becomes. Likewise, the more we ask each other week after week, "How can I help you in prayer" (and then pray), the more natural it becomes for us to pray out loud with people. As we then head back into our everyday lives, we are better trained for seeking God's kingdom, telling our Jesus-stories (witness) and praying with people who need it so badly.

"Good Questions" help us to personally rediscover the goodness of the Good News: As we sort through our experiences and share our stories as Missional Community, we start to clarify and simplify for ourselves what is so good about the good news of Jesus. In other words, we start to find words and stories that personally and concretely express what Jesus means to us. And that's gold, because when we find the words and stories that express the goodness of the good news from our own lives, we can start sharing that good news with those who need it so badly.

A tip for getting started with "Good Questions": If your Missional Community is like most, during the first few gatherings, the group may have some difficulty framing the events of their daily lives with the activity of Jesus in the middle of it. In other words, at first they may think they have no Jesus-stories to tell. That's normal. So to help them, invite the group to recall a really good or really hard interaction they recently had with someone. After they have recalled that, ask them, "And what do you think Jesus might have been up to there? Tell us the story." This will help them start connecting their real-life interactions with the real-life activity of Jesus.

A "Good Question" for the disciple-maker: Finally, there is a good question we, as the ones doing the discipling, would be wise to keep in mind as our Missional Community is arriving: "How is Jesus already discipling them today?" We do our best discipling when we join Jesus where he's already at work messing with them, wrestling with them or asking something of them. Our discipling agenda becomes whatever Jesus' discipling agenda already is. So, as they are arriving, find out what he is already up to in their lives by asking something like, "How's Jesus been messing with you this week? What questions are you asking?"

4. **All of That Is Still This**

What does "All of That Is Still This" mean? There are 66 books in the Bible. Beyond that, countless books of theology have been written. Even Luther's "*Small" Catechism* is more than 30 pages long. And it's all good. But all that theology can be overwhelming even for the academically gifted. So if our conversations start to get lost in theological complexity, we can remind each other, "All theology still boils down to this: our true identity and mission have been restored in Christ, which flows into a simple lifestyle of seeking his kingdom, humbling ourselves and freely offering to others what we have received in abundance." In other words, "All of That Is Still This."

Jesus practices something similar in an encounter recorded in Mark 12:28-31: "One of the teachers of the law came and heard them debating. Noticing that Jesus had given them a good answer, he asked him, 'Of all the commandments, which is the most important?' 'The most important one,' answered Jesus, 'is this: "Hear, O Israel, the Lord our God, the Lord is one. Love the Lord your God with all your heart and with all your soul and with all your mind and with all your strength." The second is this: "Love your neighbor as yourself." There is no commandment greater than these.'"

The answer could have been complicated but Jesus said to keep it simple. "All of That" is really "Still This."

5. **Insight to Action**

When we use the previous four practices as part of our Missional Community's reflection and conversation, important insights about life with Jesus will be prompted for each person. However, gaining insight alone is not sufficient for people to gain actual *experience* in seeking the kingdom and joining Jesus in real life. For that, they need to go *do* something. So Susan and I have learned to use a practice we call "Insight to Action." This practice gives each person the opportunity to self-identify and clarify the insights they have received during the time together. With that clarity, they then can put their insights into action during the coming week. Why is this important? Simply put, when they put their insights into action, they hit the accelerator for their discipleship training.

- **Insight + Action = Training**
  And eventually produces an experienced Jesus-follower.

- **Insight – Action = Information Accumulation**
   And eventually produces an inexperienced Jesus-scholar.

An easy way to put this practice into play is by asking, "What insight did you receive today? And how can you put it into action this week (especially for the good of others)?" With a little time to process their responses, the people head out the door with a clear insight and a simple plan of action for joining Jesus during the coming week.

One last note: Especially during the early stages of discipling, one of the most common "insights" people have is that they don't know how to do basic things like seek the kingdom, read a Bible or pray. For instance, let's say you have a new person who isn't sure about how to pray. What would you do? At first you might think it would be a good idea to find a study on prayer and go through it together. However, rather than study prayer, start praying together on a regular basis. Show them how to pray and then take turns praying. Take their insight, "I don't know how to pray," and turn it into the action of praying together. Studying prayer is good. Discussing their questions about it is good. But in the end, the most important training they can receive from you is actually praying together. With that experience, they can then practice praying on their own during the week. The same can be done with reading the Bible or seeking the kingdom.

So that is a run through the 5 Discipling Practices. These practices help Susan and me optimize the limited time we have for discipling our Missional Community. Though most of our time together is filled with unhurried conversation about the gospels and living our lives on mission with Jesus, the practices are particularly effective at framing and directing that conversation toward Jesus' discipling outcomes. After all, why whisper softly the things you want loudly to be?

HERE'S THE POINT

Though our time together in Missional Community is filled with unhurried conversation about the gospels and our lives on mission with Jesus, we have learned to use 5 Discipling Practices that help us purposefully frame and direct that conversation toward our discipling outcomes. You can think of them as best practices for your Missional Community toolbox.

CHAPTER 16
MY PLAN FOR DISCIPLING OTHERS

*"Discipling is the process of showing the people of God
how to participate in the mission of God as a daily lifestyle."*

—*From Joining Jesus: Show Me How*

So it's time to craft your plan for intentionally and consistently discipling your family and friends. You have gained clarity from the gospels about how Jesus discipled his followers. You have assembled some best practices for your discipling toolbox. Now what will your discipling plan be?

By now you know two things:

1. You want your plan to reflect Jesus' plan. (Jesus' plan for Jesus' results.)

2. You want your plan to be clear and simple so that you can be intentional and consistent in discipling your family or friends over the long run. (Clear and simple is sustainable. Unclear and complicated is not.)

Below is a template that will help you craft such a plan. Two versions of the template are provided. The first version is annotated and is intended to help you understand how the template can be used. The second version is streamlined and intended to be filled in. (The template is also available as a free download from dwelling114.org.)

DISCIPLING PLAN TEMPLATE

WHO?

Who will I disciple to join Jesus on his mission?

(Who is willing and ready? Who do you think Jesus is leading you to invite into a discipling relationship?)

- Name(s)

How will I invite the person(s) into a discipling relationship?

(See an example in chapter fourteen, "How Do I Start?")

- Write out your invitation. Be sure the expectations are clearly but winsomely communicated.

When and where will we have our Missional Community gather?

(What options are sustainable for everyone? When you find the best choice, prioritize it in everyone's calendar.)

- When:
- Where:
- Number of weeks we will meet:

WHY?

Why are we meeting? What is our discipling goal?

(Example: "Our goal is to help each other learn how to seek God's kingdom and join Jesus on his mission as part of our everyday lives.")

- Write down your discipling goal so you can remind each other of it every time you meet:

HOW?

How will I help the person(s) I am discipling engage Jesus' discipling process of Proclamation, Imitation/Participation and Replication?

My Plan for Proclamation

In the gospels Jesus begins his training process by engaging his followers with his spoken-truth. He says, "The words I have spoken to you are spirit and they are life" (John 6:63). I will facilitate the same kind of training for the person(s) I am discipling in the following ways:

1. I will ask them to take time every day to follow Jesus around in one of the gospels and take note of what he is giving them to believe and do. To help facilitate this, I will encourage them to ask themselves, "As a result of what I have received from Jesus in the gospels today, what is one thing he is giving me to believe and do?" I will do the same thing.

   - We will each follow Jesus around in the Gospel of

     _____.

     (Choose one: Matthew, Mark, Luke or John)

2. I will ask them to seek out a Christ-centered congregation every week and listen for what Jesus is giving them through its preaching and teaching ministries. I will do the same thing.

3. I will ask them to participate every week in the reflection and conversation of our Missional Community and to listen for what Jesus is giving them through the stories and insights shared.

My Plan for Imitation/Participation

In the gospels Jesus continues his training process by inviting his followers to join him on his mission. Jesus also regularly takes time to be alone with his disciples for reflection and conversation about what they are learning while on mission with him. I will facilitate the same kind of training for the person(s) I am discipling in the following ways:

1. As part of their daily lives, I will ask them to look for opportunities to join Jesus on his mission and imitate his lifestyle practices for the good of others. To help facilitate this, they can use the 5 Mission Practices and the 5 Lifestyle Practices of Jesus (see below). I will do the same thing.

The 5 Mission Practices:

- Seek the kingdom.

- Hear from Jesus in his Word.

- Talk with people.

- Do good.

- Minister through prayer.

The 5 Lifestyle Practices of Jesus:

- Remember your True Identity and Mission in Christ.

- Look for what the Father has prepared in advance for you to do (seek the kingdom).

- Submit to the Father's timing and purpose in the moment (humble yourself).

- Freely offer a little of what you have already received in abundance from the Father.

- Show others how to do the same.

2. I will ask them to regularly gather in Missional Community for reflection and conversation about what they are learning while on mission with Jesus. I will use the 5 Discipling Practices (see below) in order to frame and direct our time together.

The 5 Discipling Practices:

- Remind them of their **True Identity and Mission in Christ.**

    This is who we are. This is what we have. And this is what we do.

- Remind them that **In Here Is for Out There**.
    What we do in here with our Missional Community is for the sake of joining Jesus on his mission out there, replicating our training with others out there and eventually multiplying our group so that more people can be discipled out there.

- **Ask Good Questions**.
    We use the 5 Questions as a starting point for prompting reflection and conversation.

- Remind them that **All of That Is Still This**.
    All the many details of theology still boil down to this: we are restored in Jesus and called to imitate his simple Lifestyle Practices for the good of others.

- Give them time to plan how they can turn their **Insight into Action** for the coming week.

A Sample Agenda for Our Missional Community

- People arrive and catch up with each other.

- Find out what Jesus may already be up to by asking, "How's Jesus been messing with you this week? What questions are you asking?"

- When ready, open with prayer and restate the Discipling Goal.

- Remind each other of our "True Identity and Mission in Christ" and "In Here is for Out There." (Discipling Practices 1 and 2)

- Prompt reflection and conversation with the 5 Questions. (Discipling Practice 3)

- When helpful, remind each other, "All of That Is Still This." (Discipling Practice 4)

- Leave time at the end for the following questions: *(Break into smaller groups if you need to save time.)*

  - ✓ *"What insight did you receive today and how can you put it into action this week?"* (Discipling Practice 5)

  - ✓ *"What small part of our experience today can you replicate with your family or friends during the coming week? How did it go last week?"*

  - ✓ *"How can we help you with prayer?"*

My Plan for Replication

In the gospels the third part of Jesus' training process is Replication. Soon after he begins training his followers, we see Jesus sending them out to begin replicating their training with others. I will facilitate the same kind of training for the person(s) I am discipling in the following ways:

1. As noted above, toward the end of each Missional Community, I will ask, "What small part of our experience today can you replicate with your family or friends during the coming week?" By taking small but intentional steps like this, they steadily gain experience in how to disciple others. I will routinely ask them how it is going.

2. Over time, as their experience and confidence grows, I will help them fill out their own Discipling Plan for their family or friends so they can become even more intentional and consistent in discipling them.

3. I will help each person gain experience in leading a Missional Community by having them take turns leading our group through the agenda. I will initiate this as soon as they become comfortable with the rhythms of our gatherings. Then we will rotate the leadership role each week. The goal is to prepare them to eventually multiply and lead new Missional Communities.

4. When they are ready, I will help them begin a new Missional Community.

SUMMARY STATEMENTS FOR MISSION AND DISCIPLING

Finally, I will frequently review the summary statements below so that I can consistently bring clarity to the people I am discipling.

- **What is the mission of God?**
  According to God, his mission is to redeem and restore all things through Jesus.

- **What is our mission mindset?**
  Jesus is pursuing his Father's mission and he invites us to join him. We don't go *for* Jesus. We go *with* Jesus. He does all the heavy lifting of redeeming and restoring human lives. We just get to help.

- **How do we join Jesus every day?**
  Joining Jesus on his mission is as simple as enjoying the people around us, investing in a couple pre-Christian friends and then seeking, recognizing and responding to what Jesus is already up to in their lives. The 5 Mission Practices and 5 Lifestyle Practices of Jesus help facilitate this.

- **What is discipling?**
  According to Jesus in the gospels, discipling is the process of showing the people of God how to participate in the mission of God as a daily lifestyle.

- **What are we discipling people to do?**
  We disciple people to participate in the mission of God by imitating the simple, redemptive Lifestyle Practices of Jesus (see the list above).

- **What is our discipling curriculum?**
  Our discipling curriculum is to watch Jesus, imitate him and practice what he shows us over and over again. There are

three sources for watching and imitating Jesus: 1) the life of Jesus in the gospels; 2) our life with Jesus every day; and 3) the examples of other experienced Jesus-followers.

- **How do we disciple people?**
  We invite people to join Jesus on his mission and help them engage his discipling process of "Proclamation, Imitation/ Participation and Replication."

DISCIPLING PLAN TEMPLATE

(The template is available as a free download from dwelling114.org)

Who?

Who will I disciple to join Jesus on his mission?

- Name(s):

How will I invite the person(s) into a discipling relationship?

- Write out your invitation:

When and where will we have our Missional Community gather?

- When:
- Where:
- Number of weeks we will meet:

Why?

Why are we meeting? What is our discipling goal?

- Write down your discipling goal:

How?

How will I help the person(s) I am discipling engage Jesus' discipling process of Proclamation, Imitation/Participation and Replication?

My Plan for Proclamation

1. I will ask them to take time every day to follow Jesus around in one of the gospels. I will do the same thing. We will use the Gospel of _____.

2. I will ask them to seek out a Christ-centered congregation every week and listen for what Jesus is giving them through its preaching and teaching ministries. I will do the same thing.

3. I will ask them to participate every week in the reflection and conversation of our Missional Community and to listen for what Jesus is giving them through the stories and insights shared.

My Plan for Imitation/Participation

1. As part of their daily lives, I will ask them to look for opportunities to join Jesus on his mission and imitate his lifestyle practices for the good of others. I will do the same thing.

2. I will ask them to regularly gather in Missional Community for reflection and conversation about what they are learning while on mission with Jesus. I will use the 5 Discipling Practices in order to frame and direct our time together.

My Plan for Replication

1. Toward the end of each Missional Community, I will ask, "What small part of our experience today can you replicate with your family or friends during the coming week?" I will routinely ask them how it is going.

2. Over time, I will help them fill out their own Discipling Plan for their family or friends.

3. I will help each person gain experience in leading a Missional Community by having them take turns leading our group through the agenda.

4. When they are ready, I will help them begin a new Missional Community.

CHAPTER 17
PERSONAL PRACTICES FOR THE WISE DISCIPLE-MAKER

"Follow my example, as I follow the example of Christ."
—Paul in 1 Corinthians 11:1

If someone has learned a lesson the hard way, you can trust their wisdom when they offer it. And if *many* people have learned the *same* lesson the hard way, you are wise indeed to pay *very* close attention to it.

The following wisdom was learned the hard way… by many people.

Making disciples is simple, but it can also be hard—especially in the beginning when we are still relatively inexperienced. Even when everyone is on board and has the best of intentions, we can find ourselves quickly burning out or wandering around in a discipling wilderness wondering what went wrong. That's why we are wise to listen carefully to disciple-makers who have gone before us and take up their personal practices as our own. Their wisdom was earned the hard way and is of great value.

So if you don't want to end up being a disciple-maker who is burned out, wandering endlessly in the wilderness or quitting in discouragement, then you will want to be sure to do the following for yourself:

1. Fully engage the lifestyle you are discipling others to live.

2. Continue *being* discipled by an experienced Jesus-follower.

3. Honor God's rhythm of work and rest.

As a disciple-maker, these practices are the difference between living on fumes and living in fullness. By heeding this wisdom, you will be blessed and so will the people you are discipling.

1. **As a disciple-maker, be wise and fully engage the lifestyle you are discipling others to live.**

    On the one hand, it's so much easier to coast. It's so much easier to talk about joining Jesus than it is to actually do it. But on the other hand, what does that gain us? We can't lead others where we're not going and we can't show others what we're not doing. So, because the ones we are discipling need to see in us the fruit of following Jesus, we quickly come to a fork in the road: we either fake the fruit (and our soul slowly withers as a result), or we fully engage a lifestyle of following Jesus so we have authentic fruit to show (and we live from abundance as a result).

    The choice is clear: Fake it or follow Jesus. Live on spiritual fumes or spiritual fullness. Coast and wither or allow Jesus to keep giving us more, telling us more and showing us more as we follow him and join him on his mission? (See Matthew 13:52.)

    Here is wisdom: We are already discipling our family and friends *to receive from* Jesus in the gospels, *to join* Jesus in everyday life and *to be encouraged by the examples* of others in our Missional Community. Why not simply grant yourself the same grace and participate in the same lifestyle? You gain both fulfillment as a Jesus-follower and fruitfulness as a disciple-maker. Don't settle for faking the fruit of following Jesus when he's inviting you to participate in the real deal... for your sake as well as the sake of those you are discipling.

In the end we are simply following the wisdom that Paul shared long ago: "Follow my example," he said, "as I [continue to] follow the example of Christ."

2. **As a disciple-maker, be wise and continue being discipled by an experienced Jesus-follower.**

I have asked my daughter Emilie to share with you some of her hard-earned wisdom about following this practice. She is a millennial, a beloved daughter of the Heavenly King and a disciple-maker at a church plant in Knoxville, Tennessee:

> *I used to think I was a stories person. I thought I could talk to any human for hours and happily be engulfed by their stories and joys and hurts. Of course I would interrupt often for quips and stories of my own, but that was only for the noble reason of enjoying the sound of my own voice and having hilarious and wildly intelligent things to say. So, really, you're welcome.*
>
> *But y'all, this lady was different. She was not even stopping to breathe. Trust me, I know, because I had been anxiously awaiting a pause for at least 15 minutes—any pause at all that I could leverage to get out of this story, this conversation, this endless monologue.*
>
> *But it turns out, this lady wasn't different. Instead I felt my eyes glazing over in one encounter like this after another for*

weeks. People and their stories went from fascinating me to boring me to, worst of all, annoying me.

"Oh, you want to talk too? Fine, it's not like I have anything better to do. Sure, keep talking like my only job in the world is to hear the sound of your voice. Let me guess, you have something to complain about? Ah, yes, what a surprise."

I work for a church. I am supposed to disciple people. I am supposed to actively care for people. At the very least I am supposed to politely listen to their stories without becoming an irritated zombie.

Yet an irritated zombie, I was.

I was reading my Bible. I was attending church. Heck, I was working for church. I was surrounded by reminders and requirements and words that pointed me to Jesus.

These are good things. But I learn time and time again (yes, I enjoy learning the same lesson eight or nine times before moving on to something new) that these are not the only things.

This world is broken. The longer a person lives in this world, the more their body and mind begin to deteriorate. We humans do not naturally flourish. None of us were ever designed to grow and thrive by just powering through life in this broken world. No, it claws at us. And if we're pouring into other people without a Jesus-following mentor and community pouring back into us, the claws will start to get to us. The world will start to drag us down. And even if we're listening and giving and helping with the best of them but "have not love, [we are] a noisy gong or a clanging cymbal." When I stop taking my own discipleship seriously, it is only a matter of time before I stop loving well and taking the discipleship of others seriously.

In order to engage with stories, help with hurts and disciple others, we need to not just read our Bible and go to church, we need the grace of someone discipling us too.

It is not biblical to disciple without being discipled. It is not sustainable to disciple without being discipled. It is not fun to disciple without being discipled.

So let's not, shall we?

[You can read more of Emilie's writings at meanderingsandramblings.com.]

Emilie is spot-on. We are wise to seek out an experienced Jesus-follower who can regularly pour into us and disciple us even as we disciple others. Who is that person for you? Who can encourage you but also challenge you to keep learning and growing? Who has disciple-making experience that he or she can use to help you stay on course as you disciple others? Who can bring objectivity to your journey when you feel like you're going to go crazy? Having such a person keeps you humble, hopeful, teachable, and accountable as a disciple-maker. In a word, such a person keeps you *healthy*.

The discipling relationship of Timothy and Paul is a great example for us. Paul had discipled Timothy since he was a young man (see Acts 16:1-5). At first Paul considers Timothy to be like a son (see 1 Corinthians 4:17), but soon, as Timothy is discipled in the ways of Jesus, Paul also calls him a brother (see 2 Corinthians 1:1) and a coworker (see Romans 16:21).

Paul trusts Timothy so much he eventually sends him to disciple the Corinthians, Philippians and Thessalonians in his place (see 1 Corinthians 4:16-17, Philippians 2:22 and 1 Thessalonians 3:2). However, even though Timothy is discipling many other people, he continues to *receive* discipling from Paul so he can keep growing as a Jesus-follower and a disciple-maker himself (see 1 and 2 Timothy).

Who can be your Paul?

3. **Finally, as a disciple-maker, be wise and honor God's rhythm of work and rest.**

    Susan and I have tried insanity. It is overrated.

    We are both high-energy, high-capacity, goal-oriented people. We both are passionate about Jesus and the redemption and restoration of people he is pursuing. And if we are not very careful, we can be working hard for the cause of Christ all the time. All. The. Time.

    But living that way *in the name of* Jesus is not *the way of* Jesus. That pace, intensity, and burden are both insane and unnecessary. Jesus says it this way in Matthew 11:28-30 (MSG): "Are you tired? Worn out? Burned out on religion? Come to me. Get away with me and you'll recover your life. I'll show you how to take a real rest. Walk with me and work with me—watch how I do it. Learn the unforced rhythms of grace. Keep company with me and you'll learn to live freely and lightly."

    As Jesus-followers and disciple-makers, there is a rhythm we can learn: we work hard with Jesus and then we rest well with him too. We see Jesus honoring this rhythm in the gospels as he personally works hard but then gets away to rest with his heavenly Father in prayer (see Mark 1:32-35 and Mark 6:45). We also see him honoring it as he manages his followers (see Mark 6:31).

We are wise to do the same.

Unfortunately, in the 21st century, Jesus-followers have largely forgotten how to take a real rest with Jesus. And as a result we have also lost track of how to live freely and lightly with him. We are chronically intense and chronically exhausted. For many of us, "rest" has become a four-letter word. We equate resting with wasting time. But in the Bible, God equates resting with wisdom. He designed human beings to be at their best when they have both meaningful work and restorative rest. Our mistake these days is that we routinely dismiss the value of rest rather than honoring it as a key part of our design. We do this in spite of the fact that one of God's Ten Commandments is for us to work hard for six days but then to rest from work for *one full day*. And did you notice how he built a hard-start and hard-stop into the rhythm of each workday? They are called "sunrise" and "sunset." His design is that we get up with the sun and work hard. Then we wind down with the sun and rest well with family and friends. While working hard is important for being productive, so is resting well. Of course, resting well is not just for restoring our energy for work; it is also for restoring our energy for people.

So, if we are coming to our discipling relationships exhausted and running on fumes, who are we benefitting? Violating God's design for work and rest is ultimately unsustainable and unwise. We break down. And exhaustion is certainly not a fruit of the Spirit. Instead we are wise to grant ourselves the grace of regular rest with Jesus.

And that begs the question of *how* do we rest with Jesus. Rest is not just ceasing from work. Rest is better than that and more than that. Rest is ceasing from work so that we can be refreshed, restored and reenergized. But *by what*? As Jesus-followers, we might guess that the answer is supposed to be "Jesus." But do we actually feel that way? Does spending time with Jesus sound to you like a great way to rest? Or does it sound to you like more work?

And here is where the breakthrough can happen: Have we mistaken *religious obligations* for *being with Jesus*? That is exactly the misunderstanding from which Jesus is setting us free in Matthew 11 above. Religious obligation is endless work. Being with Jesus is our source of refreshment, restoration and energy. When Jesus is working hard in the gospels and then ceases so that he can go be with his Father in prayer, he doesn't say, "Oh, great. I have one more thing to get out of the way before I can rest." No. Jesus is going to be with his Father so that he *can* rest! "Finally! I can take a breather with you, Father, and let you refresh me and renew my energy. I'm whipped."

So if resting with Jesus doesn't sound too restful, then maybe your "relationship" with him is really nothing more than a "religious obligation" to him. Instead receive Jesus' invitation *out* of that way of thinking, "Are you tired? Worn out? Burned out on religion? Come to me. Get away with me and you'll recover your life. I'll show you how to take a real rest." We don't need a rest *from* Jesus; we need a rest *with* Jesus. We don't need to get away *from* Jesus; we need to get away *with* Jesus. "[Come with me and] learn the unforced rhythms of grace. Keep company with me and you'll learn to live freely and lightly."

Of course different people are refreshed differently. Some are refreshed in nature. For others, it is in a room full of books or a room full of people or a room full of music. Find your way and enjoy it often.

And finally, a word about honoring this rhythm as a Missional Community. We regularly gather in Missional Community because Jesus set the pattern for his disciples in the gospels. Gathering like them is healthy for us and an expression of rest with Jesus. So, most of the time, the most fruitful way to honor God's rhythm as a group is by gathering. But there are also times and seasons when the most fruitful way to honor it is by *not* gathering. Follow the lead of Jesus. Guard against having a legalistic and rigid attitude about your schedule for gathering. Life happens and Jesus is in the middle of it. Have grace for the ebbs and flows of how life goes during the year. During some seasons you may meet every week for months on end. During others, you may only meet occasionally. Either way, remember, Missional Community is an expression of rest, not obligation. Or to borrow from Jesus, "The Sabbath was made for man, not man for the Sabbath" (Mark 2:27).

So how will you honor God's rhythm of work and rest going forward?

HERE'S THE POINT

As a disciple-maker, if you don't want to end up burned out, wandering endlessly in the wilderness or quitting in discouragement, then here are three personal practices you would be wise to follow. You will be blessed by them and so will the people you are discipling:

1. Fully engage the lifestyle you are discipling others to live.

2. Continue being discipled by an experienced Jesus-follower.

3. Honor God's rhythm of work and rest.

A FINAL WORD

And now you're ready.

We have clarified what a disciple is and how to make one according to Jesus in the gospels. You now have a discipling plan that reflects his plan and a toolbox full of discipling tools. You are ready to begin discipling your family and friends intentionally and consistently.

So all we have to do is put it all together, and—abracadabra!—we'll have ourselves a disciple of Jesus, right? Well...

I have a friend who likes to say, "All we can do is bring the water. It's up to Jesus to turn it into wine." That's certainly true of discipling. I need to do what Jesus gives me to do. I have my part to play. I get to help. But in the end, it is still Jesus alone who works the miracle of transformation in a person's life.

You might have recognized that my friend's quote is a reference to the wedding at Cana recorded in John 2. During the wedding, Mary tells Jesus the wine has run out. In response, Jesus eventually tells the servants to fill six large jars with water. Each jar could hold 20-30 gallons of water. And the servants do it. In fact we are told that they fill each jar to the brim. (Do you think they knew Jesus was up to something?) Then Jesus does what only Jesus could do. He changes all the water into wine. Really good wine.

And so it is as we disciple our children, neighbors or fellow church members. We follow Jesus' discipling plan. We do what he tells us to do and fill each jar to the brim in anticipation. But in the end, all we can do is step back and enjoy the way Jesus turns all that discipling water into discipling wine. His miracle of transformation may happen quickly or slowly; it may happen smoothly or by fits and starts; it may be inspiring or frustrating. But let's follow the advice of Mary, who said to the servants, "Do whatever he tells you."

BENEDICTION

And now it's time for you to go and start making disciples of your family and friends.

Jesus says to you, "As the Father sent me, I am sending you." But he also says, "Let not your heart be troubled." He is sending you, but he is also going with you and leading you. "Come, follow me."

Jesus isn't asking you for your flawless perfection, only your humble participation. Keep it simple. Be intentional. Be consistent. You bring the water. He'll turn it into wine. So review your discipling plan, take a deep breath of prayer and start inviting your family and friends into a discipling relationship with you. Some will say, "No," but some will say, "Yes," and then the adventure can begin!

Now go, in the name of the Father whose mission it is to redeem and restore all things, in the name of the Son who is pursuing his Father's mission and inviting you to join him and in the name of the Holy Spirit who is enabling you to show others how to do the same. Amen!

JOINING JESUS—SHOW ME HOW:
HOW TO DISCIPLE EVERYDAY MISSIONARIES

"The main thing is to keep the main thing the main thing."
—Someone who has discipled people before

This Discussion and Implementation Guide is designed to help you process and implement insights gained from reading *Joining Jesus—Show Me How.* The book has two parts. The first part takes you back to the gospels so that you can watch Jesus and clarify in your mind how he disciples his followers. The second part helps you leverage this clarity in order to craft a simple plan that you can use to disciple your kids, willing friends and neighbors or fellow church members.

As you begin working through the guide, take note of the following:

1. If you are unfamiliar with the mindset, practices and support advocated in Greg Finke's first book, *Joining Jesus on His Mission,* take time to review the executive summary provided at the end of the introduction.

2. For Session 1 (below), if you are reading this book as a congregational leadership team, start with question #10 and then continue with question #1 and following after that.

SESSION 1: WHAT IS DISCIPLING ACCORDING TO JESUS?
(CHAPTERS 1-2)

The goal of this book is to help you regain the clarity and simplicity of how Jesus disciples people in the gospels so that you can disciple your children, friends, neighbors or fellow church members to join Jesus on his mission too.

1. Consider your family and close friends. Each of them needs ongoing discipling (training) to be a follower of Jesus in everyday life. Does the idea of you discipling them make you nervous? Where do you think the nervousness comes from?

2. Did you have a "blinding flash of the obvious" while reading chapter one? What was one insight that you especially appreciated?

3. What are you looking forward to as we work through this book together?

4. Chapter two begins by clarifying what the word *discipling* means. What insights did you gain?

5. Why is it important to keep our understanding of mission and discipling clear and simple?

6. What is *discipling* according to Jesus in the gospels? The author suggests one way of summarizing the answer. How is that summary helpful to you?

7. What are the four things we learn about Jesus' discipling process from Matthew 4:19? Did any of the four surprise you?

8. C. S. Lewis once observed that being a great theologian can easily be mistaken for being a good Christian. What do you think he meant by that? What is the caution he is offering to

us as we move forward?

9. What is one insight from today's discussion you can put into action in the coming week?

10. For Congregational Leadership Teams:

Take a moment to reread the "Note for Church Professionals and Congregational Leaders" in the book's introduction. Then discuss the following before going to question #1 above:

a. What discipleship dreams do you have for your congregation?

b. What do you like/not like about this statement: "You can't develop an effective system for discipling a whole congregation until you have experience effectively discipling an individual person."

c. "Disciples are not mass produced. They are handmade." Why is this statement accurate? What challenges/ opportunities does it offer your congregation?

d. What are some of the keys to seeing a mission and discipling movement emerge from your congregation? Where does such a movement start?

SESSION 2: WHAT IS THE MISSION OF GOD ACCORDING TO GOD? (CHAPTERS 3-5)

1. Why is it so important to be clear about what the mission of God is?

2. According to God, what is his mission (and, therefore, our mission)?

3. The author walks us through the reasons why God made us

and saved us. What are three points that stand out for you and why?

4. What is our small part of God's great big mission? How does this insight help you?

5. What if all the people in church worshipping Jesus this Sunday went home and loved their neighbor? What difference might we see?

6. Can you name a friend or family member who is living without the grace and truth of Jesus?

7. What is his/her story—how did they grow up; what were their circumstances; what happened to them?

8. Chapter five suggests that we are under-discipled (undertrained) for personal participation in the mission of God. Why do you agree or disagree?

9. If we are currently under-discipled when it comes to important priorities like joining Jesus on his mission and discipling others to do the same, how can we get more fully trained by Jesus?

10. Did you learn anything new about your baptism while reading this section? If so, what?

11. Why is it so important for us to get off the bench and actually join Jesus on his mission if we want to receive a higher level of training?

12. What is one insight from today's discussion that you can put into action in the coming week?

SESSION 3: HOW DOES DISCIPLING WORK? (CHAPTERS 6-8)

1. What is "the rub"?

2. According to Jesus, what does "becoming like him" look like?

3. How does Jesus change us through discipling?

4. How did you react when you read "what baptism gives, training now matures"?

5. What did you like about the Pizza Ranch story?

6. How would you describe what discipling looks like?

7. What made sense as you read the section about Matt and Casper?

   The author suggests that "discipling plans" generally fall into one of the following categories: scholarship, membership or relationship. After which plan do you want to model yours? (In chapter sixteen you will have the opportunity to craft your own discipling plan.)

8. What qualifies us to disciple others?

9. What did you like about this section? What challenged you?

10. What is one insight from today's discussion you can put into action in the coming week?

SESSION 4: WHAT IS A DISCIPLE AND WHAT DOES A DISCIPLE DO? (CHAPTERS 9-10)

1. The question is asked, "If we're supposed to make disciples, what is one?" Where is the best place to go for our answer?

2. The author suggests the following summary definition for what a disciple is according to Jesus:

A disciple follows Jesus:

- in order to become *like* Jesus (through baptism *into* Jesus and training *by* Jesus);

- so that he/she can participate *with* Jesus on his mission as a daily lifestyle;

- and show others how to do the same.

What is helpful about this? As you read the gospels, do you think anything needs to be added to this summary?

3. The author unpacks "what a disciple is" in light of what Jesus shows us in the gospels. Were there any "blinding flashes of the obvious" for you? What challenged your previous assumptions?

4. Not all the people who were following Jesus around in the gospels were disciples of Jesus. What made someone a disciple?

5. The question is asked, "How in the world can we be like Jesus?" What is your answer?

6. Toward the end of chapter nine, it reads, "Turns out, discipling people to be followers of Jesus is less about mastering libraries of theology than it is about mastering a few simple practices for the good of others." Is this statement freeing for you or disturbing? Why?

7. In the beginning of chapter ten, what did you appreciate about the words of Dallas Willard?

8. The Bible gives us three main places where we can watch Jesus and imitate him. What are they?

9. In the gospels Jesus trains his followers by having them come

with him, watch him and imitate him for the good of others. What is Jesus doing that he wants us to imitate? We might presume such a list would be endless. In reality, his list is quite focused and simple. How does the author suggest we summarize the lifestyle practices of Jesus? List them below:

_____

_____

_____

_____

_____

This is Jesus' simple, redemptive lifestyle that he wants us to imitate. How would you explain these lifestyle practices to others?

10. What is your true identity, and when was it restored?

11. Why is remembering your true identity so important for your daily life?

12. What is one insight from today's discussion you can put into action in the coming week?

SESSION 5: WHAT IS JESUS' DISCIPLING PROCESS?
(CHAPTER 11)

1. What is the difference between hearing about something conceptually and experiencing it?

2. What made sense to you about the author's experience with Jon and Rob in the Golden Hill neighborhood?

3. What three words does the author use to summarize

and organize Jesus' discipling process?

How would you explain each part of the process?

Why is each part necessary to the discipling result?

4. What is a simple way to pivot from Proclamation to Imitation/ Participation?

5. What is a simple way to pivot to Replication?

6. What are the key phrases that sum up this chapter for you?

7. What is one insight from today's discussion you can put into action in the coming week?

SESSION 6: WHAT IS JESUS' DISCIPLING CLASSROOM AND CURRICULUM? (CHAPTERS 12-13)

1. What two discipling "classrooms" do we see Jesus using in the gospels?

2. Why is it important to pay attention in the "classroom of daily life"?

3. The author calls the "classroom of time together" *Missional Community*. Why did Jesus use this kind of classroom?

    What are some ways we can engage Missional Community?

    Which seems like a good fit for you?

4. What benefits do questions like the 5 Questions provide to a Missional Community?

5. What is the primary difference between a Missional Community and any other small group or Bible study?

6. What is the specific curriculum that Jesus uses to train his followers?

7. Where are the places that the Bible gives us for watching and imitating Jesus?

8. What are the strengths of using written materials?

   However, if we want to use Jesus' *full* curriculum in order to disciple our family or friends, what else do they need in addition to written materials?

9. What part of Jesus' discipling curriculum takes the most effort and investment?

10. As you look at the suggestions for building a close relationship with the people you are discipling, which ones stand out for you? Which challenge you?

    What changes will you need to consider in order to make room in your life for this kind of relationship with family or friends?

11. The author points out that many will struggle with the idea of someone "imitating" their life. What encouragement and reminder does he offer?

12. What is one insight from today's discussion you can put into action in the coming week?

SESSION 7: WHAT IS YOUR DISCIPLING PLAN?
(CHAPTERS 14-17)

Having gained clarity about the way Jesus disciples his followers in the gospels, you can now imitate him as you craft your own discipling plan.

1. Getting started: The author offers several best practices in chapter fourteen for starting well. Each is important. Which one stood out for you and why?

2. Optimizing your time in Missional Community: The best opportunity you will have for discipling family or friends is during your Missional Community time. Because this time is limited, it is important to optimize it by using the 5 Discipling Practices described in chapter fifteen. Each is important. Which one stood out for you and why?

3. Crafting your plan: chapter sixteen presents a template for crafting a plan for discipling your family or friends. If you haven't done so already, take time to fill in the template now. Then review your discipling plans with the others in your group. What questions do you still have? What are you excited about?

4. Staying healthy: chapter seventeen presents three personal practices for the wise disciple-maker. Each is important. To which one will you need to pay particular attention in the months ahead?

As you close, read together the final Benediction.

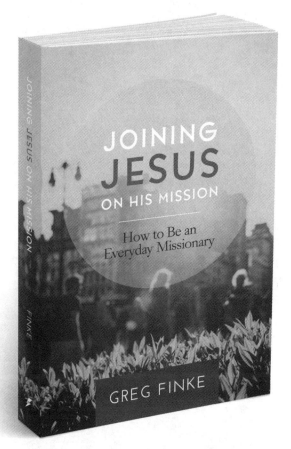

JOINING JESUS ON HIS MISSION:
How to Be an Everyday Missionary

Available in print and e-book formats (Spanish and English) at online retailers. Visit www.dwelling114.org for more information regarding audio, video curriculum, and quantity discounts.